W9-BLP-636

Red Hugh,
Prince of Donegal

Also by Robert T. Reilly

FOR YOUNG PEOPLE
Massacre at Ash Hollow
Come Along to Ireland
Rebels in the Shadows

FOR ADULTS
Irish Saints
Christ's Exile

red hugh
prince of donegal

robert t. reilly

O'Donnell

BETHLEHEM BOOKS • IGNATIUS PRESS
Bathgate, N.D.   San Francisco

© 1957 The Bruce Publishing Company
© renewed 1985 Robert T. Reilly

Cover Illustration © 1997 Gino d'Achille

Cover Design by Davin Carlson

All rights reserved

First Bethlehem Books edition, September 1997
Second printing, July 1999
Third printing, May 2001

ISBN 1–883937–22–1
Library of Congress Catalog Number: 97–73495

Bethlehem Books • Ignatius Press
10194 Garfield Street South
Bathgate, ND 58216
www.bethlehembooks.com

Printed in the United States on acid free paper

Red Hugh,
Prince of Donegal

fOReWORD

"A TALE THAT IS not told dies." That's what
the old Irish storytellers like to say as they
light their clay pipes from the turf fire and launch
into a fanciful report on the legendary ghosts of their
region or the "little folk" that do be bothering the
lonesome traveler.

But sometimes their story is true—as this one is.
And evenings when the embers are smoldering and
the crickets scuttling among the warm ashes, the
ancient Gaelic narrators hold their audiences spell-
bound with the tale of *Red Hugh O'Donnell.*

Red Hugh lived at a time when the first settlers
from the Old World were eyeing the new conti-
nent, America. Shakespeare was writing his great
plays and England defeated the Spanish Armada to
become "Mistress of the Seas." During his lifetime,
gunpowder was to become more prominent as a
weapon of war and, less than twenty years after his
death, the Pilgrim Fathers would land on Plymouth
Rock.

His mother, Ineen Duive, was one of those remarkable warrior queens for which Ireland is famous.

Her exploits serve to place her beside the fabled Maeve and Scota. But she had her gentle side, one that was in keeping with the true chivalric spirit of Ireland during those years.

On the Elizabethan maps, the gallant MacSweeney appeared as two crossed battle-axes, the symbol of his military might. His loyalty to his neighbor in Donegal is spoken of proudly by those who prize such virtues.

Every royal family had its own poet or shanachie and in Martin of Cloghan we shall find all of the features of the true bard. Contrary to current belief, the poet was not a weak and feminine man whose verses were his single attribute. He was often a fine warrior who rode into battle with his lord.

Villains there are, too, in this old tale. The English viceroys bore the brunt of the Irish hatred but behind all of their scheming rises the figure of Elizabeth, the powerful sovereign of that age.

Elizabeth never met Hugh Roe O'Donnell face to face but, in the events that closed both of their lives, they would learn much of each other. During the famous Nine Years' War which follows the tale you are about to read, O'Donnell and his ally, O'Neill, defeated every army sent against them and turned back the invader on every front. Their defense of their country is one of the noblest chapters in this world's short history.

But that's another story—one that has a grown

man for its hero. Our hero is yet a boy. The crickets have ceased their chirping and the shanachie has plucked a flaming straw from the warm turf. I believe he's about to begin his tale.

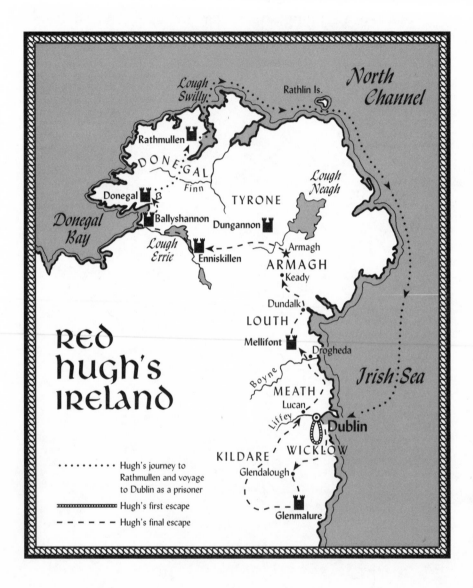

North Channel

Lough Swilly

Rathlin Is.

Rathmullen

DONEGAL

Finn

Donegal

Ballyshannon

Donegal Bay

Lough Errie

Enniskillen

Dungannon

TYRONE

Lough Neagh

Armagh

ARMAGH

Keady

Dundalk

LOUTH

Mellifont

Drogheda

Irish Sea

Boyne

MEATH

Lucan

Liffey

Dublin

WICKLOW

RED HUGH'S IRELAND

KILDARE

Glendalough

Glenmalure

· · · · · · · · · Hugh's journey to Rathmullen and voyage to Dublin as a prisoner

▨▨▨▨▨▨▨ Hugh's first escape

– – – – – Hugh's final escape

chapter 1

IN THE FAR west of Donegal, where the waters of Lake Eske plunge headlong into the Atlantic, a solitary castle stood guard over a quiet September. Shaped like a sledge it was, with the massive head facing the stream and the long row of stone dwellings forming a handle that stretched to the opposite wall. Low-lying heather and tiny firs dotted the courtyard and repeated the triangular pattern which marked the gabled rooftops. The fortresslike head rose four stories high and towered above the rest of the buildings. Each corner was the base for a turret and the largest of these faced the ocean. There were few windows and these were but wide enough to accommodate the archers.

Surrounding the entire structure was a bawn, a large space enclosed by a stone wall. Within this lived the servants and retainers whose thatched huts ranged around the entire perimeter of the castle. Cattle were sheltered here at night and here, too, was the exercise and game area for the peasants and their lords. The bawn was quiet now. An old man could be seen carrying some turf into his hut and a little girl drove some sheep past the fortress and across the drawbridge to pasture land. A blacksmith's hammer sounded rhythmically from his shop and a score of busy looms wove a melody about the smithy's cadence.

From the ramparts of the castle the restless sentries swept the steep banks of the river and, behind them, armed warriors paced warily along the crest of the broad enclosure. Bowmen stood guard over the land approaches and a few small ship's cannons pointed their iron muzzles toward the open sea. Powder and shot stood nearby and rack after rack of pikes and axes gleamed in the warm autumn sun. If the bawn displayed a people at peace, the fortress disclosed a people ready for war.

And well might the archers be alert and the bold infantrymen, or "gallowglasses," at their posts. For this was the year of our Lord, 1587, and the bright, broad shield of the O'Donnell looked down from the parapet above the moat.

On this stone shield a plump, brown wren roosted, cocked its tail, and then blinking beneath its white brows, sailed into the courtyard and peered boldly from its rock sill at the woman who lodged within.

Ineen Duive O'Donnell, queen of the northern clan, turned for a moment toward the small bird and smiled. Then, placing the palms of her hands against one another, she pressed her slender forefingers against her lips, musingly closed her eyes, and turned slowly back to the men that sat around the table.

Anyone observing her, as she faced the brehons, the Gaelic judges, would note first the deep, jet eyes and the ebon hair that settled easily on her white neck and shoulders. It was these features that had earned for her the title of "The Dark Lady of Donegal." She was a tall, intense woman whose proud carriage and regal presence informed the observer she was born to the throne. She was of the Scottish MacDonnells but had left her homeland years ago when the king of her Irish kinsmen had married her amid the swirl of the pipes and rollicking, kilted dancers. Now Hugh, her husband, was a bedridden invalid and to her fell the task of leadership in the stormy province.

"It is true," she addressed them, with her eyes half shut, "it is true that my son may not please all that meet him nor stir in them the conviction that he should be king. But king he shall be, nonetheless, and the time may be upon us for the crown to pass from his father."

A white-bearded ancient who propped his weary body against the heavy table spoke up for the judges. "Arrah, my lady, it is not that the prince is not well liked. By the saints, the reverse is true. The people love him. But he is young and has the faults of the young."

The queen lifted her head. "Hugh is fifteen," she replied. "My father ruled his clan at that age and I, myself, rode into battle when but a year older."

"Aye," another of the lawgivers interrupted, "it is

not the age alone. If you will excuse an old man, we all fear the young prince is impatient and headstrong and not much given to the serious aspect of things."

The Dark Lady smiled patiently. "He is also courageous and clever. You have said so yourselves."

The first brehon made a searching little gesture with his hands and sucked in his breath before he spoke again.

"We know that the English Queen Elizabeth has promised to destroy us. Hour does not replace hour but we are made aware of her threat. Do you think young Hugh can manage her? Can he organize a defense as well as govern a province?"

"I shall be with him in his early years and his father has the wisdom to guide his footsteps."

The brehons exchanged a look of disbelief.

"His father is still the king," she reminded them sharply. Then softening, she added, "And there is the prophecy to consider."

The three judges nodded wearily and the youngest, who had not spoken, said, "The people here believe it, but a prophecy is not proof against Elizabeth's fleet or her armies."

The queen seated herself at the head of the council table and rested her strong hands on the arms of the oak chair. Behind her, on the rippling arras, were emblazoned in gold the words, "O'Donnell Abu," "O'Donnell to Victory," the battle cry of the clan.

"It was first proclaimed by judges like yourselves," she said at last, "and the legend has swept like a flame across this green land until every hut and every castle wills that it shall come to pass." Her brow furrowed as if she looked past the silent elders, past the dim hanging lamp, and beyond the dark paneled chamber that enclosed the present. "It was said," she continued, "that when Hugh succeeded Hugh, then should Ireland be free. And now, in this generation, does my son Red Hugh sit at the knee of his father, the old Hugh O'Donnell, my husband. When he shall leave that place and seat himself on that timeless throne, then shall the words of ages past be redeemed. We shall see it happen."

There was a long silence in the room, until one of the judges began to speak again.

"My Queen," he said gravely, "do you not think that Elizabeth, too, knows the prophecy? Do you imagine for one whisper of a moment that, cunning as she is, she will see this transpire without a battle?"

Ineen rose, her long garments trailing behind her, and walked again to the window where she allowed the wren to peck at her fingers.

"Och, she is cunning, right enough," she said, smiling, "and schooled in the arts of deceit and intrigue. They say she wears a red wig and has many lovers who flatter her and call her beautiful. Her galleons choke the channel and her warriors mock the challenge of Spain. And yet does she fear me—for I have a son!"

The impertinent little bird scolded the queen for her laughing pride and the old brehons took her bright reverie as a signal for dismissal. The wren wheeled about the fall sky inventing idle melodies. Their complaints expressed in noiseless gestures, the lawgivers drifted back through the cold, dim halls of the castle.

chapteR 2

THE HOODED FALCON let out his cries of "Kak-kak-kak-kak" as he was carried through the woods. The accompanying horsemen—the young red-haired, blue-eyed youth whose shoulder served the bird as a perch and the older man with the pale, thin face and cap of sparse white hair—chatted as they rode. Two Irish wolfhounds loped obediently behind, eyeing the four rabbits that hung limply from the youth's saddle.

As every forest bird and beast could tell, this was Hugh Roe O'Donnell—Red Hugh—and his shanachie, the learned Martin of Cloghan. Every noble family in Ireland had its brehons, its poets and harpers, and it had its shanachie whose job it was to relate the tales of the ancient heroes. These stories young Hugh never tired of hearing and thus Martin was a frequent companion. At times like this, when the hunt was over and the prince returning to his home, he would plague the storyteller with questions.

"And was Cuchullain never afraid, then?" the boy asked.

The shanachie turned easily in his saddle and his

face brightened with the drama of the story he was about to tell.

"Of course, of course," he said. "Each man fears something. Cuchullain was no different. Och, I could tell how he trembled once so that the Curlew Mountains shook rocks upon the cattle grazing beneath. But it was not for himself the hero feared. Not for his own life."

Here Martin paused for a moment but Hugh did not interrupt. He smiled eagerly, knowing a story would follow. A flock of redpolls flew overhead and the blindfolded hunter went "Kak-kak-kak-kak" again. The breath of a breeze spilled the brown leaves before them as Martin continued.

"Aye, it was during the terrible wars as between the Red Branch Knights and their enemies from Connaught. Then it was that the great champion, Cuchullain, stood by the north bank of the river that split the warring clans and defeated all that came against him. Bold champions of Connaught—Calatin, with his seven and twenty sons, and Fraech, son of Fidach—all dropped before the sword of Cuchullain."

The names fell more softly on the boy's ears than the drifting leaves.

"Then"—and Martin stretched his hands as if to silence the forest noises—"ah, then it was that Ferdiad, the childhood friend of Cuchullain but now under the banner of Connaught, stepped to the riverbank and vowed he would kill the Red Branch knight." He shook his head slowly from side to side as if to say, "What a horrible thing," and let the scene take life in the mind of his listener.

Martin continued, almost sadly. "Nor could Cuchullain dissuade Ferdiad from fighting by reminding him of their comradeship when they were learning the art of war from Scathach in Alba. 'We were heart companions, companions in the woods,' he told him. 'We slept in the pine forest after mortal battles abroad.' But Ferdiad would have none of it and he cast the first spear at his friend."

The shanachie's arm thrust forward suddenly in keeping with his tale and the fascinated prince watched the phantom shaft dart across the ancient river.

Martin's voice became louder as he described the fight. "All day they fought, each wounding the other many times, but at nightfall they embraced and exchanged medicinal herbs and food and their horses were in the same stable that night and their charioteers at the same fire. Thus again the next day they fought and again that night camped together. But on the third night they bedded each with his own army for they knew in grief that one would die the next day."

"How is it, good Martin," Red Hugh asked, "that Cuchullain could not kill this man as he had the others?"

"Musha, easy that is to tell, my prince. For not only did Ferdiad know the same tricks of warfare as his companion but he was also dressed in horned-skin armor."

"Ahh," Hugh sighed and nodded in approval.

They left the woods to pace the strand that led along the sea edge to Donegal Castle. Flawless as new wheat was this sand—without a stone or pebble to mar its yellow finish. To their right the salt water whitened in surf about a hundred small islands and to their left the beach rushed against the weatherworn cliffs. The mist rolled about the top of the black crags disclosing gulls and gannets plunging and whirling in white confusion and filling the vast amphitheater with their squalling voices.

Martin rode, looking straight ahead, with his expressive hands gripping the saddle post.

"Well, that night was the one of which I told you. Cuchullain shuddered at the prospect of killing his friend, but his charioteer, Laeg, called him a coward and said Ferdiad would throw him as the river spews foam, and pierce him as the ax the oak. This brought the warrior to his senses and in the fight the next day he killed the challenger from Connaught amid the blood-red stream. Then Cuchullain took his companion in his arms and laid him gently on the bank and lamented thus, 'There has not come to the gory battle, nor has Banba nursed, nor has there come from sea or land, of the sons of kings, one of better fame.' "

Hugh looked down upon the sallow beach and then back at his friend, but he said nothing. They passed in silence a group of peasants gathering seaweed for their fields and some happy fishermen dragging their small currach to shore. The falcon twitched nervously and Hugh clucked to him. The sand was hot and the weary hounds looked longingly at the water.

"What do you think, Martin?" Hugh asked at last. "Was Cuchullain right in killing his friend?"

The white-haired shanachie pinched his lips with his thumb and forefinger as he answered. "To be sure. Else there would be fewer tales of Cuchullain, now, wouldn't there?"

He looked at the boy and saw that he was regarding him closely, waiting for the serious answer that the shanachie should make.

Martin smiled again but spoke in a different vein.

"There are many things one must do when he leads or rules that are painful to do," he said. "You, yourself, when you become king shall find many difficult tasks and you shall have to hurt others and yourself. The throne brings trouble and grief along with the glory."

"My father?" Hugh asked him slowly.

"Ah, yes, your very father, my prince. He knows what it means to rule. Now his wounds and his age keep him close-locked in his chambers. And still I believe he fancies himself at Glenmalure or Abbeyleix, his shield before him and his white stallion at the head of the O'Donnell. Och, sad it is, the fate of kings."

"Then why *be* a king?"

"Ah, indeed, why be a king is it? Might as well ask why be a gull, or a golden trout, or why be a granite streak in the Mount of Errigal. You are born to it, lad, and cannot escape it. But perhaps I have been too harsh. There is, too, the pride that rides with you before your armies and the thrill that steals upon you when the war cry of 'O'Donnell to victory!' splits your ears. Aye, there is glory—but that is but the part of it."

"It is a serious business, no doubt," Hugh said, half to himself.

The ramparts of Donegal broke from beneath the tapering cliffs and Hugh, releasing his falcon to fly along with him, spurred his horse for the castle. The ironclad hooves of his mount dug into the gilt earth or splashed recklessly through the bubbling surf. Flying straight for Donegal, the disciplined falcon paid no heed to a careless gannet whose dive into the cold Atlantic had produced a pleasant dinner item. A gull swooped to retrieve the hare that had fallen from Hugh's saddle and Martin watched him flutter about it, tearing and picking at it, a little bewildered by a mission too great for his talents.

chapter 3

"A FINE HUNTER you are," scolded the warrior who took Hugh's horse and turned him over to a stable boy.

"It was a dull day, and my bird was not himself." Hugh pointed toward the falcon circling slowly toward his wooden roost.

"Three rabbits, and small ones at that."

The remark stung Hugh who sought to excel in everything. He turned and walked away but heard the laughter that followed him. One day he would be king and then no man dare jest about his exploits.

His mother waited for him near the foot of the broad stone steps that led to the castle's main tower.

"And how was the hunt?"

The boy shrugged.

"Aha. Not good by that. Well, come, I have some news that will cheer you."

Hugh stopped plucking at his gloves and his face brightened. "What is it, Mother?"

The queen arched her eyebrows and remarked, "It will keep until I have been greeted as properly befits a mother."

The prince kissed his mother affectionately and then hauled himself up on the stone bannister, tilted his head, and dropped his folded hands between his legs.

"Well?"

The Dark Lady decided to tease him and asked in return, "What would you like most to hear?"

The boy replied quickly. "That Elizabeth's soldiers are marching north and I am to be given command of a regiment of gallowglasses."

"Hah! And what would be your next desire?" Before he could answer, the queen revealed the news to him. "The Lord MacSweeney has sent for you to attend a festival at Rathmullen."

"It *is* good news, Mother! When must I leave?"

"In the morning will be time enough. You are that anxious to leave, avic?"

Hugh put his freckled arm about his mother and kissed her again. "I shall be but a day's ride from here," he said, "and I can return quickly with the bowmen and lancers of MacSweeney. You must promise to send for me."

"Of that you may be sure, my treasure, but I do not believe the English will besiege us."

"Still I have your promise."

"Wisha, you have it in truth, but I pray no anxious rider will call you away from your holiday. Throughout the entire province MacSweeney is renowned for the magnificence of his hospitality. And, then, surely, there is Kathleen, the daughter of MacSweeney. Why, now, you may not want to return to our gloomy coast."

Hugh flushed but recovered himself and said with a low bow and mock gallantry, "Not all of Mac-Sweeney's torches, Machree, nor their reflections along the breadth of his lake, could light one of O'Don-nell's rooms as does your own presence."

His mother laughed. "Go along with you now. Save your sweet-tongued blarney for the likes of Kathleen."

The prince skipped across the courtyard, vaulted a hitching post, and started up the stairs to his father's room. Ineen Duive looked after him until her eyes met those of a disapproving brehon who had wit-nessed the scene. This ancient smiled wisely above his folded arms.

The queen tossed her head and stalked off. "He has not yet felt the crown on his head," she called to the counselor.

The well-worn stone stairway to the chamber of the elder O'Donnell wound like a coil of rope up the main tower of the fortress. Hugh paused outside his father's door and looked for a moment through the turret slit which faced west. Only fishing craft moved in Donegal Bay, some dropping their nets near St. John's Point and others heading inland from the pen-insula to the clear fresh water of the Lake of Erne. From somewhere below he heard the strum of a harp and the voice of Martin of Cloghan singing softly of

the days of Ossian when the Irish field armies strode
the forests and leaped the salmon-swift streams. In a
trice the swell of the sea and the song transported
him back to those days and he wondered if his was
the arm that would set Ireland free as they said even
then.

His meditation was interrupted by a weak call.

"Is that you, Hugh?"

"Yes, Father." Hugh turned the massive handle on
the paneled door. "I've come to say hello and good-by."

The king lay on a special couch of inlaid walnut,
covered by a quilt upon which was stitched the
O'Donnell coat of arms. From this, his workbench,
he conducted the trifling business still left to him.
For, as all Donegal knew, the once proud chieftain
managed few of the affairs of the castle. It was to
the Dark Lady that the artisans, the peasants, and
the men-at-arms looked for guidance and leadership. Her husband's long illness had weakened him
in body and in spirit. Most of his waking hours
were spent in idle planning of primitive military
tactics and the redrawing of old battle plans. Now
he lay pale and helpless beside the rough sketches
of brighter days. Yet, even in his infirmity, he drew
hope from the sight of his son and saw in him all
the dreams of the O'Donnell, all the destiny of
Donegal.

His head shook as if in continual agreement and
his hands pulled nervously at the clothing across his
sunken chest. Now and then he would cough, close

his eyes, and then quickly smile to show that it was nothing to worry about.

"Your mother tells me you'll be bound for the North in the morning, or will you disappoint Mac-Sweeney?"

"No sir. At dawn I'll ride to Lough Swilly, spend five days there at the feis, and then back to Donegal."

"Fine! Fine!" The chieftain nodded more deeply. "Do not worry about us, boy, but enjoy yourself. The queen's soldiers will not trouble our province when they hear the O'Donnell is prepared to meet them." The old man's eyes took on some of the defiance that even years of illness could not dim.

Hugh smiled patiently and sat beside his father. "I have promised my mother," he said, "that, if the English attack, I shall be in the field with MacSweeney before your messenger has dismounted."

The king's face revealed a pale attempt at a grin which disappeared in a racking cough and then returned. He embraced his son. "Kneel, boy, and take my blessing."

Next he addressed Hugh in a faltering voice. "I shall not be about when you leave, Hugh, but I shall hear your step in the courtyard and the tread of your steed on the drawbridge and shall know that you leave but for a time. When the days for the festival have been completed, then will your mother and I again listen for your cry below the gate and the castle shall feel the safer for your presence."

"Thank you, Father. And I shall convey your greeting to MacSweeney."

"Arrah, please do. And remind him that I shall be well again one day and ride there to visit with him."

They embraced again and Hugh left quickly, closing the heavy door quietly behind him. He thought that perhaps he would return a day early to please his father. He could not know that it would be many Septembers before his footsteps would re-echo on the tower stair.

But now, his duties behind him, the young prince moved from place to place in the castle, bidding farewell to Martin and others, checking equipment, seeing to his horse, and completing the packing of his leather saddlebags. Finally he was satisfied. In his simple, cold room the future king of the O'Donnell laid out his richly embossed shield, sword, hand ax, and short bow. In these weapons were all his dreams of conquest and, as he slowly welcomed sleep, he saw the armor take on an unconscious life of its own. The shield of the O'Donnell dashed wildly among the battlefields of his dreams. Shadowy imagination carried him through the perils of battle, of seething rivers, dark forests, across grim peaks, and ever and again as he forged his way he could hear the brave chorus shouting, "O'Donnell Abu!"

Outside the calm night sea fed stealthily on the Donegal shore, forming as it worked a vast setting for the dream of the dreamer.

chapter 4

THE DAY OF departure dawned with a promise
of clear weather in the songs of a thousand birds
nested in the hills. Hugh was awake early. He had
dressed in his light armor and he carried his shield
and weapons noiselessly through the sleepy gray cor-
ridors of the castle. Outside his stallion waited, paw-
ing eagerly at the earth still moist with dew.

In a moment the young lord was mounted and
the two nimble spirits, animal and human, cantered
briskly across the yard and the bawn toward the main
gate. Hugh sat rigidly in the saddle, like a king, for
he knew his father watched from the tower chamber.
The chieftain heard the clatter of the travelers on
the wooden bridge and listened until the dust of the
road had swallowed up all sound.

The sun's first rays were struggling in the rugged
landscape as Hugh rode into the hills above his home.
Donegal Bay—like a spear thrust into Ireland—the
fortress, the flaxen-roofed town of Donegal itself, the
splendid, rambling monastery—all stretched out behind him.

Soon he was galloping past the tree-fringed shores

of Lake Eske and into the horseshoe of mountains which nearly encircled it. Then Barnesmore Gap, the three miles of flanking hills whose wild appearance is broken only by the heath on the slopes and the still green banks of the little Lorreymore River which winds beside the road.

As he ambled through the foreland, his mind rushed ahead to Lough Swilly and the welcome waiting there. It was a land as familiar to Hugh as his own Donegal for it was in the north that he spent a great deal of his youth as the foster son of MacSweeney. In accordance with the custom of "fosterage," a man sent his child to be reared and educated in the home and with the family of another member of the tribe or a friendly clan. This resulted in the closest tie of friendship between the families and in all of Ireland there were no clans closer than the O'Donnell and the MacSweeney. Between the boy and his foster father, too, there existed a bond which could be broken only by death. Perhaps—and it was yet but half a thought to Hugh—perhaps someday the bond would be strengthened when Kathleen MacSweeney would become the bride of Hugh Roe O'Donnell. It was a marriage long talked over in the great halls and over the flagons of beer. But Hugh had vowed that he would wed her as king and not until then.

Startled sparrows wheeled out of the way of the sprinting horse and a few frightened deer darted for cover in the shadowy timbers. A peasant driving his thin herd of sheep waved a greeting with his staff and a sleepy Irish colleen looked up from her milking as Hugh rode past. About a circle of small bright lakes a family worked on the harvest field and an impudent spotted dog left them to snap at the heels of the travelers.

Across the bridge at the swift-moving River Finn and past the field of pale blue flax young O'Donnell moved. At the River Deele he rested his horse, watered him, and then remounted to ford the shallow stream.

By now, he had reached Letterkenny, the Hillside of the O'Cannons. Standing on the high ground above the cathedral town, he had his first view of the lough. From here he could see the winding River Swilly emptying into the lake that bore the same name and the cultivated valleys which stretched away on either side.

The prince walked his horse down the steep main street of the village and nodded in greeting to the many shopkeepers who recognized him. Before the cathedral he paused and spent a few moments with the lively bishop who blessed him and sent a greeting to his father.

Then he passed along the west bank of the lake, a fjordlike arm of the sea reaching inland for twenty-five miles between the peninsulas of Fanad and Inishowen. There was much to delight him as he made his way to Rathmullen. Each of the many sandy beaches and obscure coves recalled the sunny summer hours spent pleasantly in their waters. And the bleak cliffs and curious rock formations that rose up against the soft mountain background reminded him of the noisy sham battles fought with wooden sword and shield amid the heroic heights.

The mountains of Croaghan and Crockanaffrin bulged ahead of him and he pushed his horse to a gallop toward nearby Rathmullen. He tried to picture MacSweeney but the details blurred in his mind. He saw a huge man with a dark beard, heavy eyebrows, and with little black hairs quilled on his broad nose. He recalled the voice—deep, like the cry of a heron, and the great arms, knotted and ridged with the scars of Abbeyleix and Killaloo and other conflicts. Even in anger, MacSweeney could laugh and jest and he remembered him talking to the animals they stalked—"Ah, my pretty," he'd call softly to a twitching rabbit, "you may wrinkle your nose at MacSweeney but MacSweeney'll not turn up his nose at you." And he'd bid the deer slow down for his arrow and he'd tease the very fish in the streams. "Come now," he'd say, "we both must eat. First yourselves and then the lot of us." It was hard for Hugh to see in him the man called by all the North "MacSweeney of the Battle Axes." It was said that he could cut down a horse at one swift stroke and that his bristling blade could cleave a path to the sea through Muckish Mountain. "Sure, he's a grand man," Hugh thought. "It's lucky as a lark I am to call him friend."

A land crab gaped at the horse and rider spurting across the pebbled beach. There was a dull echo mocking them from every cliff they passed.

"And Kathleen, how will she look?" Hugh wondered. Things could change in two years. But in his young heart he knew she would be as before—a creature as fair and fascinating as the depths of the lough and, to him, as unknown. It was natural that the clans should scheme at their betrothal, and it was as natural to him that this tiny girl, this clever, charming, exasperating promise of a woman should be the bride of Donegal. The years crept back like a slow tide and washed in the present. Rathmullen's gray fortress and low-lying monastery came into view and the white cottages of the town fell into a row for a time and dispersed again. The black toe of a mountain appeared to be prodding the whole village toward the cool water.

MacSweeney's eyes were weary from watching the lake trail but now he was rewarded with the sight of his former pupil. He shouted to his charger, "Come on now, you pagan!" and rode forth, bunched on the horse like a stack of damp hay, thanking the saints in a loud voice for this day.

Ah, and wasn't there a fine reunion for the two of them. The northern giant bounded to the earth, swept the red-haired Donegal prince from his saddle, and lifted him, armor and all, six feet above the ground.

"By the powdhers o' delft, lad, you're soft. That princely livin' has feebled you surely."

For answer, Hugh suddenly dropped to the ground and yanked MacSweeney with him. Then, placing his feet in the chieftain's stomach, he thrust his legs forward and tumbled him into the shallow water at the lake's edge.

When MacSweeney emerged, dripping like a liberated amphibian, he cuffed Hugh good-naturedly and roared with laughter. "Well, it's not all you've forgotten surely. But you'll get your fill of sport at the Fair, by this blessed iron." And he slapped the battle ax attached to his horse's trappings.

When they were mounted and ambling slowly toward the town, Hugh remembered his father's instructions. "The king, my father, sends his greetings and wishes you the luck of God and the prosperity of Patrick on all that you may see or touch."

MacSweeney nodded in appreciation. "Aye, and how is the O'Donnell? Well?"

"Not a bit of it," said Hugh, "for he is confined these many years to his room and has but himself for amusement."

"A pity on it." The black-bearded chief spat. "And now the devils of English to add to his woes."

"You've heard of the queen's threats?"

"Indeed, indeed. And perhaps a bit more than you. They say Elizabeth—bad scran to the name—they say she fears you shall link arms with O'Neill of Tyrone who even now has the best army in all of Ireland."

"Sure, I've never met O'Neill, and how could I then make a pledge to him? And are you not forgetting my father still rules at Donegal?"

The chief shrugged. "That may be as it may be. I only tell you what the merchants say that put in here. They speak of Hugh Roe O'Donnell—your very self."

"And do they say the English will attack Donegal?" Hugh asked. "For already we are securing against such a day and I, myself, was a little unwilling to leave the castle."

The elder man shook his head. "Ah, I do not think it. Never a bit of it. It is a cold unwelcome place for strangers here. Donegal is no easy mark surely and they would not stand alone. Our weapons will not rust while the O'Donnell suffers. Nor do I doubt but that O'Neill would welcome the chance to be at the throats of the queen's men."

"Then what can the queen hope to gain by her threats?"

MacSweeney shrugged again, his massive shoulders thrusting the beard aside. "It's hard to outguess Elizabeth, but I would be on my guard like a grouse in a meadow. Her agents are many and I doubt but we have them even here." The chief saw Hugh's brow darken and added, "But come, this is a time for happier thoughts. We dine tonight at Rathmullen where you'll meet some old friends and then a little sleep will do you good."

The two were soon cantering across the last

stretches of the rust-colored sands and up to the castle itself. MacSweeney ushered Hugh to his room, saving the welcomes for the evening, and bade him dress for the dinner and entertainment that would follow. The prince sought to catch a glimpse of Kathleen and debated asking about her. But luck and courage both failed him and he placed his hopes on meeting her at dinner.

chapter 5

"HAVE A CARE there!" the cook cautioned the gilly who was carrying the roast pig to the table. "I'll have you on a platter should you drop that."

The timorous servant entered the banqueting hall of the MacSweeney balancing the heavy plate on his shoulder. The smell of the slow-roasted pork steeped in spices, currants, and jellies assailed his nostrils and he closed his eyes momentarily to drink in the pleasant aroma. His new-opened eyes blinked in the yellow glow of the torches sprinkled up and down the great hall. A fire crackled at the far end of the room and smoke played among the ceiling timbers. Family crests and stacks of arms decorated the walls. Flagstones at the feet of the diners and their long tables were arranged to draw attention toward the main table where MacSweeney supped in royal splendor, his family and guests to his left and right. Kathleen had not appeared as yet but a place was saved for her next to the delighted prince.

A sumptuous assortment of meats decorated the tables—beef, mutton, veal, lamb, coney, capon—and a dozen varieties of fish lay patiently in their wooden bowls. There were sweets and jellies, milk, wine, butter, cheese, and little cakes of wheat and oats. The gilly boys in their short tunics carried in dishes of parsnips, radishes, carrots, green melons late from the vines, pumpkins, beans, and roasted acorns in a steaming vessel. The clatter of the wooden utensils competed with the gay banter of the festive party and the ashen torch smoke mingled jealously with the delicate mist from the tables.

Hugh dipped his bread in the pullet broth and immersed the small prunes swimming there. Mac-Sweeney nudged him and directed his attention toward the three clowns who had leapt in from a hallway. They were clad in dark gray cloaks and pantomimed with such grace and humor that, though you sat by the corpse of a loved one, you could not but laugh.

Then followed a juggler with ear clasps of gold and a speckled white mantle. He had nine each of swords and shields and balls of gold and these he kept in the air in turn so that none fell and only one at a time rested on his palm. The sound as they passed each other was like the speech of wild flies on a summer day.

It was the harper next, and the exquisite Irish airs he strummed blended well with the company. The music alternated between fiery martial tunes and slow laments for dead heroes. Soon he was joined by the family bard who held a position similar to Martin of

Cloghan. The bard was immune from harm in Ireland and held a place in the kingdom next to that of a king. He was to receive the highest seat of honor in the dining hall and be presented the finest foods and he was rewarded with gold for the soft romantic tales and stirring ballads that he composed. His was a sacred post demanding "purity of hand, bright without wounding, purity of mouth without poisonous satire, purity of learning without reproach and purity of husbandship." Now he depicted in his fine strong voice the feats of MacSweeney of the Battle Axes.

"Hail, broad ax of MacSweeney," he sang. "Oft hast thou been on the blood-red field, oft swinging and singing and beheading high princes. Oft on the sea and in the green forest, in the banquet halls and before the eyes of thy warriors." The long tale celebrated the northern chieftain's many warlike successes and his quiet reign in time of peace. Then the poet turned with a wink to Hugh for his inspiration.

> A sweep and bow to the Prince of Donegal,
> Flaming sword of the West,
> Brother to the brilliant sun,
> Who comes as welcome guest
> To our blue lough.
> His shield the shield of kings,
> His smile all friendship brings
> And perhaps some other things
> To the heart it dare unlock.

To the closing phrase the poet added a nimble little dance step and laughingly retreated. Amid the general hilarity he returned and grinned innocently at the boy. MacSweeney dismissed him with the gift of a gold flagon and the harper took up his lonely chore.

Suddenly a hush fell over the hall. Even the snapping fire seemed to diminish. Kathleen, the daughter of MacSweeney, entered the great room. She was Hugh's age but carried herself with the strength and dignity of a woman. Her ebon hair hung loosely and she was dressed brilliantly in a gown of gold brocade. Laughter played along the edges of her gray eyes and tugged at the corners of her coral mouth. Her gaze never left her father as she tread lightly across the flagstones, spoiled a little, perhaps, but in command of this moment.

When she had come to the seat next to Hugh she extended her hand for him to kiss. Arrah, many a man would have stood there then to have that white hand in his. Hugh felt the flush rise to his face as he gulped a salutation and awkwardly stumbled back to his chair and upset his wooden plate. MacSweeney enjoyed his predicament to the utmost and directed many a good-humored jest his way. But Kathleen, ever the lady, twinkled inside and preserved an outward air of perfect deportment.

So the meal wore on with MacSweeney reciting for his company the embellished stories of Hugh's fosterage. Nor were these unpleasant to the prince's ears, for thus does love like to speak, though in accents not its own.

"By the blood of Clontarf," the chieftain said, "when I first took young O'Donnell there in hand, it was little hope I had of making a soldier of him." He paused and affixed a broad smile to the sentence. "Now I see that I was right." In this way MacSweeney teased him and Red Hugh colored and wondered if Kathleen pitied him.

When the bowls were removed and the goblets of wine presented with a "Slainte!" for all to share, Hugh and his childhood sweetheart stole to the balcony of the great hall. Lough Swilly, distended before them, looking surprised at its own silver and purple majesty. It was as if the moon had slipped up in one swift movement and thrust a spear across her undulating waters.

None could tell what the young lovers discussed. For the surf lapping at the shore of the lake, the soft-stringed discourse of the harpers, and the clink and cackle of the great hall drowned out every other sound. We may be sure they talked of the future and Kathleen saw the mantle of a king resting on Hugh's shoulders in the moonlight. And he saw her as his queen looking down from the towers of Donegal at the muffled lash of the Atlantic. And thoughts of numberless tomorrows flew as echoes of that instant to the surrounding hills.

When the hour for retirement crept upon the hall, touching first the sputtering fagots and expressing itself in yawns and nods, all were sorry to leave such gay company. Even the guests whose tired limbs recalled the day's travel were reluctant to follow the solemn torchbearers to their quarters.

Hugh lay awake for a brief time listening to the faint sallies of the lough, the song of a vagrant linnet, and the orchestral monotony of myriad crickets. It seemed a thousand years and a thousand miles from Donegal. Thoughts of Kathleen were uppermost in his twilight reverie. What was it she had said to him? First she teased him and said he did not care since he had not visited her in more than two years. And she imitated his awkward way when he greeted her and scolded him anew for ignoring her these many months. But she grew silent when he spoke to her of his studies for the kingship and his hopes for the throne of the O'Donnell. It was then she told him, "When you go to seek a queen, do not neglect to search these hills. I have a prophecy of my own invention to fulfill." He feared this girl outmatched him in wisdom and she frightened him a little. But he could not forget the sight of her when she walked into the great hall and the torches dimmed and the fire burned low and the music melted into the gray walls.

Soon, lulled by song and shadow, the young lord fell asleep. The morning was upon him before he awoke and he heard a cock crow in another world. But he was soon dressed and joined Kathleen for the journey to the Fair grounds. The dark-haired girl clung tightly to her escort's arm as they moved among the festive crowd to the lake's edge.

There was much to delight the eye and ear and much to attract the heart and charm the will. Jugglers controlled the course of dozens of painted objects and street fiddlers struck up lively jigs. They gave forth with the withy dance, the sword dance, and the difficult "rinnce fada" or long dance. Peasant couples cast off their cares with their shoes and pranced in the dusty arena. Boiling pots of salt beef and strong-smelling cabbage hung between the tents and the first beakers of ale were being filled.

This was a time for serious business, too, and cattle and sheep and a few horses were on hand for the trading that should commence as soon as the crowd had arrived. Every visitor wore his or her finest in jewels and gold, and not a thief was there to bother them, for such was the tradition of the Fair.

"Oh, look!" said Kathleen, drawing Hugh aside.

Two beggars were leading a tired nag at the end of a dirty string and asking for gold. Hugh threw them a shilling and received both a grateful smile from his beloved and the yellow-toothed thanks of the suppliants.

A little puppet play was being enacted and Hugh and Kathleen dallied there. Then they moved on past a group of children munching grapes and spitting the seeds into the lough. For a time they applauded the musical antics of a piper no older than themselves and followed the course of a dozen races, watching the bold horses darting in and out of the black coves

that unsettled Swilly's coast line. To be alive this day
was worth a month in battle, for the hills echoed and
the waters quivered with the sounds of laughter and
poetry, of song and trade—all the acoustics of the
Irish fair.

To the far end of the area the two young people
walked.

"Do you be having these fairs often?" Hugh asked.

"Not but once a year. Do you not have them at
Donegal?"

Hugh shook his head. "Not since my father has
taken ill. There is not the heart for it in our people."

"Will you not enter in the games here then?"

Hugh's face brightened. "I will, to be sure. I see
there is wrestling here and the sticks are primed for
hurley. Ah, but first, I do want to run my horse in
the races. You'll not be lonesome?"

"Aye, that I will be, but it is best I let you join in
the sport or they shall say I've bewitched you into a
pale figure of a man."

"Then 'tis the truth they will be telling."

Hugh ran to the spot where his horse was teth-
ered. He raced and rode with the finest men of the
North and many an honor fell to his fleetness and
skill. Kathleen stood by and watched and she watched,
too, as he dominated the game of hurley, an ancient
sport not unlike hockey. He dashed back and forth on
the field, his hurley stick flashing in the sun and the
black ball darting before him. When he sat down to
rest with his broad chest heaving, Kathleen prodded

him to his feet and dragged him off to witness the
Fair's main event—the casting of the mighty hammer.

It was in this event that MacSweeney was undis-
puted champion and from his tutor Hugh, too, had
learned to master the sledge. A bright red stake had
been driven in the ground far from the throwing
ring to mark the record heave of the northern chief
set six long years ago. The mark was challenged by
many of the eager young men but all casts of the
massive hammer fell short of MacSweeney's stake.

"Are you going to try?" Kathleen asked Hugh.

The prince shook his head.

"Go on," urged the girl. "You can do no worse
than the others. Come! I'll hold your things."

Hugh laughed, shrugged, and handed her his jacket
and side arms. When he stepped to the circle a little
ripple of excitement ran through the crowd for here
was the pupil trying to outdo the master. Despite his
youth, the Donegal prince was one to be reckoned
with because he had the physique of a man and he
had been drilled in this exercise many a day during
his fosterage.

Hugh's first toss was farther than that of any other
competitor but still short of the stake. He rested a
moment, lifted the sledge, placed his foot on the
starting mark, swung the heavy instrument back and
forth twice and then, whirling in a complete circle, let
fly with it. The hammer left his arm like an arrow
from a bow and sped in a bright arc toward the goal.

Kathleen gasped and the spectators swallowed her little cry in a great shout. Hugh, tottering on one leg,
saw that the sledge had struck the red stake and shattered it. He had tied the record!

Puffing and panting, he stepped back to Kathleen. A hundred hands reached out to congratulate
him. But the contest was not yet over. The rules
permitted the old champion one more throw. The
chieftain removed his cloak and shirt and handed
them to a friend. Standing thus before the assem-
blage he drew a burst of applause. In the prime of
life, MacSweeney was the picture of vigor and determination as he strode to the broken stake and
recovered the hammer. Then he took his place in
the throwing circle.

A hush came upon everyone so that the wash of
the lake could be heard for the first time that day.
Even the circling gulls kept the silence and watched
the strange scene below. The very air hung heavily,
sensing the downfall of a champion. MacSweeney
had been a younger man when he established the
mark and it seemed unlikely that he could equal the
exploit of this earlier day. One throw had to do it.

None could tell what thoughts were in Mac-
Sweeney's mind as he grasped the hammer, but they
saw him swing it lightly to and fro like a painter
brushing a broad canvas. The muscles of his arms
tightened, ridging the dark skin, and suddenly he
spun around and shot the weight through the air.

He smiled slowly as he watched its flight until it

fell beyond the useless stake. The throng broke into a loud cheer for the victor and not the least of the rejoicers was Hugh Roe O'Donnell who was glad to acknowledge himself second to such a man.

While MacSweeney left to celebrate with his companions, Kathleen and Hugh continued through the Fair. Abruptly their walk was interrupted by a voice calling Hugh's name.

The call was from a little walnut-colored man who sat by a tattered tent where a sign advertised that fortunes would be told for a price. "Red Hugh O'Donnell," he repeated and signaled with a crabbed finger. "Come and I will reveal your future."

Kathleen shuddered and placed a restraining hand on Hugh's shoulder.

"I believe not in your magic, old man," Hugh said curtly, "nor do I desire to part with my gold to hear things only God can know."

The old man laughed. "Ah, do not be too sure. Sometimes the power is given to others." His right eye had a tic which wrinkled the corner of his mouth. "Will the young lord be staying with us long?"

"Not that it concerns you, but I shall be here through the five days of the Fair. Why do you ask?"

"Call it an old man's curiosity. Had you only some of this same curiosity I might predict your destiny. There will be trouble in your life."

"That hardly comes as a surprise." Hugh smiled with a glance at Kathleen.

"And you shall have a sea voyage."

The prince laughed. "So I was told once before by one of your kind and I ended fishing off St. John's Point."

The ancient one arose and bared his yellowed teeth. "You may laugh now, my pretty, but dark days shall come upon you and your merriment shall die in the advent of pain. Your eyes shall see sorrow and your nostrils smell death. You will grow weak and pale and your enemies shall feast on your infirmity."

Hugh flushed with anger, his blue eyes narrowed, and he shouted, "Enough, old fool, you forget yourself! Your age saves you from the same fate you foretell for me. Take your trade to others who will pay to be cheated!"

All atremble herself, Kathleen led him away to cool his anger, but Hugh had no stomach for the Fair after that incident. The yellow grin haunted him and the words of the prophecy chilled his soul. In his mind he could see the "tic-tic" of that diseased eye and all appetite for amusement was destroyed that day.

chapter 6

BUT FOR THREE days the Fair continued, and Hugh and Kathleen went back each day to drink in all of its blatant pleasures. The fortuneteller had since departed so that no ugliness was left to bother the happy pair. They came to know every booth, every game, and every wandering minstrel. Like sunny youngsters, with the world locked in the encompassing hills, they forgot all but each other.

On the fourth day MacSweeney suggested that Hugh accompany him to the Carmelite monastery which lay back in the hills but a few minutes' walk from the fort. The monastery was a favorite retreat for the pilgrims of the province and Hugh himself had studied here under the tutelage of the White Friars. Kathleen was left behind pouting as the boy and his foster father departed on foot for the sacred place.

Friar Thomas was pleased to see Hugh again. The priest was a huge man, larger in stature than Mac-Sweeney, and his gentle gaze overlooked a gruff countenance where a crag of a nose and a blunt mouth reviled a rosy complexion. A dozen wisps of hair, and that was all, lay on his head like wheat on a rock. He had remarkable hands and punctuated every phrase with them. Holding them before him now in mock surprise he answered Hugh's initial question, "Why, for sure it is I knew you were here. Didn't the people tell me and them late-coming from the Fair where you threw the sledge so well. It is a fine thing to have this strength. The Lord has blessed you, boy."

Hugh smiled and MacSweeney placed his hand affectionately on his shoulder.

The priest glanced sidelong at him and rubbed the nape of his own bronzed neck. "My, yes. It is the same attention you've given your catechism these years, I'm after hoping."

Hugh looked up, bit his lip searchingly, and recited, "For as lightning cometh out of the east and appeareth even in the west, so shall also the coming of the Son of man be. Wheresoever the body shall be there shall the eagles also be gathered together." He paused and squinted to recall more of the passage. "Then," he said, "there's something about 'He shall send his angels with a trumpet and a great voice; and they shall gather together his elect from the four winds' and then—no—'then shall all the tribes of the earth mourn; and they shall see the Son of man coming in the clouds of heaven with much power and majesty.'" Hugh looked pleased with his effort.

The cleric chuckled. "Good, good! Very good! And

very like Hugh O'Donnell to remember that passage. But don't you be forgetting that Matthew also says, 'I come not to destroy but to fulfill.' " And he winked at MacSweeney.

They strolled about the monastic grounds nodding to the brown-robed friars who were busy at their tasks. Each garment seemed a little more threadbare than the last but the white mantle each wore gleamed in the sun. Those cheerfully digging in the ribbed soil nodded and said, "Benedicite." While these worked the land for their sustenance, others pruned the fruit trees or tended the roses that clung to the chapel. "For," Friar Thomas would say, cupping his hands, "these flowers, too, are from God. It is well we feast our eyes as we do our stomachs." A tiny monk on a ladder was carving the twelfth station along a pebbled path and, through a stained-glass window, they could see other shadowy figures at work copying manuscripts.

"It is fine to be busy doing the Lord's work," the Carmelite reminded them. "Not, God save us, that we begrudge the life of the Fair, although"—his eyes twinkled—"I'd much like to try my hand at those games myself. But the Lord's will be done." And he looked up as if the momentary lapse from spiritual motivation needed an apology.

By now the friends had reached a little knoll which gave them a view of the simple cluster of monastic buildings, the fortress, the swirling Fair ground, and the ample lough washing the foothills. MacSweeney spoke of the Fair for a time and Hugh was silent turning over a question in his mind. At last he expressed it.

"Father, is it wrong I should wish to be king? Is it against the will of God?"

The literal MacSweeney seemed surprised by such a query but Friar Thomas knew the boy and answered him patiently. "Sure not, my son," he said. "For you remember that St. Paul tells us, 'Let every soul be subject to higher powers; for there is no power but from God; and those that are ordained of God.' And he informs us that 'princes are not a terror to the good work but to the evil.' "

Reading the troubled look on Hugh's face, he added, "You should rejoice that God has given you this opportunity to serve Him. Good will come of it, I'm sure."

"Sure, 'tis a fine day for theology," put in MacSweeney, "but look yonder and ye'll see something that delights me own untrained mind."

As they followed his directions they perceived a swift merchant ship with high poop deck and square bulging sails skirting the little Rathmullen peninsula.

"She'll drop anchor at the fort, mind ye now," MacSweeney remarked as he arose. "Come on, then, we'll see what she has to sell."

The friar blessed the two of them and taking Hugh's hand in both of his wished him well all the days of his life. Then the dark chieftain hurried his young charge out of the shadowy solitude of the monastery and across the sand-flecked shore where a small crowd was already gathering.

The ship flew an English flag but carried no armament. A few sailors could be seen parading on her deck or scurrying to lend a hand while the anchor was lowered into the lough. The frolicksome spectators awaited the landing with merry expectation. Not that there was any love lost between the people of this part of Ireland and the English. But the natives were usually willing to make an exception in the case of a merchantman, for such a vessel might well be laden with just the right amount of food and drink and splendid gifts to round out the brimful span of the festival. At the very least, the sailors would have news to impart to the welcome ears of these North country people.

A small boat had put off from the ship and was soon beached under the skillful eye of the ship's mate. With one of his typical broad gestures, MacSweeney was already wading into the shallow water with a word of greeting for the ship's company. The mate returned the greeting and reported that the ship carried a cargo of fine Spanish wines and sweetmeats from the Indies.

"And they're all for sale, sir, to you and your good people." The ship's officer winked a mirthless wink and added, "It's sad the Spanish were to lose them but more's the profit for us, I say."

"Then do be bringing them things ashore," MacSweeney said. "You've picked a ripe good time for your trading for I'm feared the poor people have their heads filled with a thousand things they can little afford."

The officer started back to the launch and then turned back. "Lor'," he said, "I near forgot. The cap'n would be obliged should you dine with him this night. And yer friend there, too, if he's so inclined." And he pointed to Hugh.

MacSweeney answered for both of them. "We'll be here come sundown and wait for your wee boat. Meantime, do make yourselves at home and it's welcome you are to anything this poor land can offer ye."

Throughout the day the small launch plied back and forth from ship to shore delivering the rare merchandise and returning Irish gold to the ship's coffers. A makeshift market was established on Swilly's west shore and the visitors from the neighboring provinces swarmed about the stand seeking an opportunity to purchase the English items.

Kathleen protested mildly at being left alone again but she did not wish to run counter to her father's plans. And so, at dusk, MacSweeney and Hugh arrived at the beach. Behind them burned a hundred campfires far up into the foothills of Knockalla and the music of a hundred Gaelic fiddlers drifted down to the calm surface of the lagoon. The Fair was coming to an end and tonight the darkness would be filled with sounds of song, laughter, and dancing, and the gleam of the distant fires would compete for hours with the lake of reflected stars. It is no wonder that Kathleen was unwilling to spend such a night alone. And Hugh felt a little twinge of guilt creep upon him. "Well," he thought, "I shall spend tomorrow with her and not leave until the next day."

The waters were gently disturbed again by the arrival of the launch and the two stepped into the small boat and put out from shore. The ship was anchored at some distance but the sounds and scenes of revelry were audible and visible to the English sailors leaning wistfully over the ship's rail. MacSweeney and Hugh were assisted onto the deck of the merchantman and received there by a tall, pale man who introduced himself as the ship's master, John Bermingham out from Plymouth. He had but the trace of a beard and his thick hair was cropped short so that its full shape was visible above the high white collar and red cloak which marked the captain as one inordinately successful in his trade. His velvet doublet and rich leggings gave further evidence of good fortune. He had a quick smile that flashed on and off like the beam of a firefly and Hugh noted that he constantly scratched his ears which had been pierced for earrings but now bore none.

Nothing else stirred on deck. A few sailors were asleep in the gangway and the helmsman lolled about on the upper deck. The only real signs of life came from the distant shore.

The captain was very gracious. "I should very much like to show you my ship after a bit," he began, "but perhaps, first, you gentlemen would partake of our table. I'm afraid naval fare is not the finest but we shall do our best." He clucked nervously and rubbed his ear with a thumb. "This way, please."

The captain directed them below to his cabin where the steward had set places for the guests and for the other ship's officers who were waiting for the visitors. Pleasantries were exchanged once more and the group sat down to eat. Hugh looked curiously after the departing steward. The captain noticed and asked, "Is something wrong, sir?"

"No. It's just your steward. He looked familiar."

"Oh? Not likely you'd know him, sir. This is the old man's first trip. Spent the most of his life in London. Maybe you been there?"

Hugh shook his head. Then he shrugged and gave his attention to the broiled fish which the ship's cook had tried vainly to embellish with some carefully placed carrots and small brown potatoes. Mac-Sweeney, whose tastes were not delicate, had already devoured his portion and was helping himself to a second dish when the master proposed that they drink a toast. The guests arose with the ship's company and raised their goblets in anticipation of the captain's words.

The same quick smile darted across the features of Captain Bermingham and his eyelids fluttered nervously. Then he recovered and spoke deliberately. "I give you the health of all those loyal to the queen and drink to the death of Ireland."

Neither of the guests moved nor raised his cup. For a moment nothing could be heard but the creaking of the vessel as it softly rolled in the lagoon. Then the clink of armor and the muffled steps of intruders sounded in the gangway.

Hugh dashed his wine at the nearest officer and rushed for his sword which he had hung carelessly on the wall. With a roar of pain and anger, Mac-Sweeney overturned the table and grabbed one of the heavy oak chairs as a weapon. The twin doors to the cabin burst open and a score of armed men poured in. The prince swung one of the English lieutenants into their path and unsheathed his weapon. The tight little cabin throbbed with the blows and shouts of the combatants.

"Easy, me bucko! Make for the door. I'll hold them," MacSweeney yelled as he cracked a skull or two with the chair. Two luckless heads fell into his hands next and he banged them together with a vengeance. More soldiers clambered into the room and the dark warrior went down under a host of angry Englishmen.

Hugh had cleared a circle of death about him but could not free himself from the persistent attacks that backed him to the wall and thwarted his escape. His lightning-quick thrusts earned him the respect of the enemy and they backed off momentarily. The prince lunged at the closest attacker but stumbled over a fallen soldier and, when he had but risen to one knee, he felt the blow of a heavy object. The captain had felled him with a lantern! His last vision was of the little walnut-colored steward that puzzled him and in that instant he remembered. The fortuneteller at the Fair!

Now the master, nursing a bleeding scalp wound, bellowed, "Clap them in irons and drag them on deck! Get ready to weigh anchor!"

When the prisoners awoke they were chained to a bulkhead and the bandaged captain surveyed them from his perch on the wheelhouse.

He smiled and said, "Ah, well now, that's enough exercise for tonight, what? Let us talk a while."

MacSweeney regarded him grimly. "What have you in your foul mind, you black-souled creature?"

"All in good time, in good time. First, an introduction is in order. I believe young O'Donnell has made his acquaintance but allow me, nevertheless, to present Master Timothy Dudall of Dublin and, I might add, a loyal servant of our gracious queen."

Before he had put in his appearance from the captain's cabin, Hugh knew that Dudall, the steward, and the fortuneteller were all the same!

"You see, gentlemen," the captain continued, as Dudall looked calmly on the proceedings, "I was but hired for this voyage. It is to Master Dudall that you owe your capture. 'Tis his mission keeps you here."

MacSweeney spat. "Then, MASTER Dudall, might

I ask you what you want of us—me and the young O'Donnell here?"

When Dudall spoke he had none of the cackle in his voice that marked the fortuneteller. It had been a clever impersonation. "Of you, sir, we want nothing. You might have spared yourself the aches of the struggle below decks for it was ever our intention that you should go free."

"And what of Hugh here?"

"Ah." Dudall raised his finger. "Now there is another matter. The O'Donnell boy stays with us to the end of our journey."

Now Hugh spoke up. "You will understand my curiosity, I'm sure, but where am I to go and for what reasons?"

"Both good questions, young O'Donnell, and both deserving of answers. We are bound for Dublin where you will remain in our custody."

"You have not stated the reason for all this—the charge," MacSweeney reminded him.

The captain standing to one side laughed dryly and dragged furiously at his ear. Dudall glanced at him and then answered, "Suppose we say it is for the good of the kingdom and to the advantage of our queen to have such a troublemaker confined. This way we can keep our eyes on him and see that he stays out of harm's way and out of ours."

MacSweeney nodded. "Sure and who would be behind this but Elizabeth. It was said she feared

Hugh would align himself on the side of the O'Neill against the English. Believe me, then, and this is as true as the sun to the dial, such a thought never entered this boy's mind."

"Perhaps not," the little old man returned, "but it might. And this way we have the guarantee that it will never develop beyond the planning stage. Clever—you must admit that." He chuckled softly.

"You shall not hold me in Dublin," Hugh boasted. "I will not be caged like an animal but shall escape and return to Donegal. Mark you that! I shall be revenged for this!"

Dudall ignored the prince and continued his conversation with MacSweeney.

"We regret that we had to infringe on your hospitality in order to carry out our mission but this had been planned long ago and the Fair seemed the best place to fulfill the assignment. We waited at the mouth of the lake until we were sure of our quarry and then we decided to attend your little gathering."

"So, that's the reason for the fortuneteller."

"Exactly, and I do believe I make a rather fetching fakir. I shouldn't wonder if I take up the practice of magic and such as a future livelihood."

The crew laughed at the comic suggestion and their leader joined them.

MacSweeney's eyes smoldered and he tensed his broad muscles within the iron bands that held him. "I believe we have heard enough," he said with finality.

"Indeed, indeed," said Dudall. "Unchain the bearded one and, bowmen, train your weapons on his heart should he entertain any rash ideas."

Four archers drew their strings and leveled on MacSweeney as his bonds were loosened. Several soldiers stepped forward and grasped his arms.

"Throw him over the side!" Dudall commanded and he waved a mock farewell to the chieftain.

As he was dragged across the deck MacSweeney called over his shoulder, "Courage, lad!"

It took six of the sailors to hoist him to the rail and dump him into the lough. MacSweeney bobbed above the waves and rolled over on his back to watch the ship.

"Help him along to shore now," the ship's captain called to the archers and they released their arrows. The water boiled around the chief with the hiss of the missiles and he struck out strongly for shore.

"Up the anchor!" Bermingham ordered. "Helmsman, bring her about and head for the sea."

The trim craft turned, caught a lively breeze, and spurted into the outbound channel. Left behind was a tired old man, wet and wounded, who lay on the beach and watched helplessly as his young charge was kidnaped. All about him rang the sounds of merriment while he wept long and without shame.

The fiddlers were closing out the Fair with the old ballad which began, "Five thousand farewells to

the arm that was round me and will not be again!"
The flame was failing in a hundred campfires and
the stars swam drunkenly in the wake of the departing vessel.

chapter 7

THE MERCHANT ship sped on through the
mouth of Lough Swilly and turned east past
Malin and the cliffs of Inishowen. Below decks Hugh
languished in his chains, filling the daylight hours with
vain schemes and sleeping fitfully through the nights.
By great limestone cliffs they sailed and skirted headlands jutting out into the boisterous sea. The captive
peered through a seam in the vessel at the lava-formed
pillars of the Giant's Causeway and the red and black
ledges that overhung it. The full fury of the Atlantic
swept them through the three-mile channel which
separates Rathlin island from the mainland and at
length they veered south past the granite walls of Fair
Head, a plateau of scrub grass and heather fronted by
fantastic gray islands of rock. Lurigedan, a flat-topped
table mountain, loomed like a draped coffin as the
merchant ship cruised along.

The captain checked on Hugh from time to time
but the boy never saw Dudall. Occasionally this
man's voice was heard as he called attention to the
tidy white town of Glenarm or when he complained
of seasickness as they fought a storm off Donagh-

adee. The scenery softened as the days wore on and now the caressing foam crept up to the roots of the warm coastal hills where the land was neatly tilled and dotted aimlessly with cottages. Here and there a castle brooded over her tenants and an orchard edged down to the ocean in a futile escape from the autumn-tinted woods. The scent of blossoms sometimes found its way to Hugh's prison in the hold and he knew that they were not far off shore. Fishermen hailed them in a friendly fashion and once Hugh saw a maiden in a wind-blown apron carrying a bucket across the strand. When they left the North Channel, the weather turned against them once more and swept the merchant craft far from shore into the Irish Sea. For several days they labored to bring the ship to starboard and finally, as the sun broke through, the lookout spied Dublin Bay sentineled by the rocky headlands of Howth and Bray Head. The ship dropped anchor into the mirror of the city's towers.

The captive, pale from his confinement and blinking in the fierce light, was brought on deck, still in irons, and was transferred to the landing boat. The oarsmen pulled steadily for land and delivered up their prize to a waiting detachment of soldiers. As Hugh fell in with them he noted that Dudall had disembarked from a second longboat and was following at a distance, with two ship's officers beside him.

Hugh had often heard his foster father speak of

Dublin. " 'Tis a dark and gloomy city, it is," Mac-Sweeney had told him, "and not somethin' the likes of you would be wantin' to spend any time in. Sure, the place is so pushed and packed that a man can scarce draw a decent breath."

And now he was here, though not of his own choosing. As he was marched along the cobbled road to Dublin Castle, people poked their heads from windows and doorways and craned for a peep at the captive. Hugh carried himself as a prince of Donegal should and many's the soul that was moved as they observed his proud red head held aloft amid the gleaming pikes. Even now the boy began to study the landmarks of the town so that he might one day use them should a means to escape present itself. But, from all he had been taught, he knew this would not be easy. The area around Dublin, called "The Pale," was in complete and absolute control of the English. Here most of their armies were quartered and here the state representatives of Elizabeth sat to plot against the chieftains of Ireland. Any prisoner who fled this trap would need friends, money, luck, and more than a little touch of Divine Providence.

From the docks it was not a long journey to Dublin Castle. The English soldiers escorted Hugh, clumsy with his chains, along the north bank of the Liffey which cuts the city in two like the blade of an ax. Across a narrow stone bridge they went and right up to the castle itself.

Dublin Castle served a multiplicity of purposes. It

was part military headquarters, part political headquarters, and part prison. A cluster of ugly, leaden
buildings grouped themselves around a pair of court-
yards and this was the entire architecture of the place.
Each corner of the enclosure was flanked by a round
tower rising high above the sloping roof of its adjacent building. Long spired columns decorated the
grim walls of the fortress and a deep and dirty moat
surrounded it. The circular towers were surmounted
by low notched parapets behind which stood the
watchful archers. A barracks for the garrison lay at
one edge of the castle and a number of its soldiers
patrolled all approaches. A threadlike stream ran
through the yard and, after passing through and
feeding the moat, fled in relief to the River Liffey
and thence to the Irish Sea. Built three centuries ago
as a Norman stronghold, the old buildings still presented a forbidding front to anyone contemplating
attack from without or escape from within.

The heavy log drawbridge was lowered to admit
the detachment and they marched in silence across
the muddy courtyard and up to the main building of
the English prison. Once inside, Hugh and the accompanying party mounted a massive central stairway
which led to the "great hall" of the castle. Hugh's first
glance at the hall took in the lofty paneled ceilings
and the gallery of paintings that strung along the oak-
ribbed walls. At the far end of the room he saw a
small figure, richly dressed, seated behind a mahogany

desk. The soldiers propelled him rudely in this direction and the seated figure rose in greeting.

Sir John Perrot, the English viceroy, was a detached and preoccupied man. As he rose he looked at Hugh briefly, paced slowly about his desk, and then sat down again. His ringed fingers drummed nervously on the mahogany.

"Welcome to Dublin Castle, Master O'Donnell," he began. "I have the honor of being your host." There was no enmity in his voice, no sarcasm. Hugh was but one of the problems of state that troubled him.

The boy inclined forward in returning the greeting but his eyes disclosed his hatred.

Perrot met his gaze and smiled as a teacher smiles at an unruly student. He introduced himself. "I am Sir John Perrot, her Majesty's servant, Viceroy of Ireland."

The prince stared at him but said nothing. His chains rattled ever so slightly on the pitted floor. The viceroy gave a little grunt of amusement and dropped his chin into his hand.

"I trust we shall get to know each other well during your stay here. I shall warn you that you will be treated fairly just so long as you abide by our rules and do not attempt to hinder the performance of our duty, try to communicate with your friends, or to escape. The latter course, I might advise you, is foolhardy. No one has ever escaped from the castle and

I do not believe my men will permit so valuable a prisoner as Red Hugh O'Donnell to mar that record."

Hugh broke his silence. "May I ask for what offense I am thus confined?"

"Simply this," Perrot replied without a hint of irritation, "that you were born an O'Donnell and that you were unfortunate enough to have as your neighbor such a man as the O'Neill. It is said that this chieftain is casting shot and storing up firearms and it is said further that the family of O'Donnell supports his activities."

"As to the last," Hugh answered sharply, "it is a lie. Between our families there is no alliance, nor had we considered the need for one until now."

"This may be as may be," the viceroy agreed in a disinterested tone. "Yet our queen has asked that we have hostages against such an alliance and it is our intention to fulfill this command to the letter." His birdlike eyes blinked slowly indicating boredom with the entire proceedings. It was of a bird that he reminded the prince—a frail heron with beady orbs, thin neck, and a long barb of a nose. And the suggestion of plumage was furnished by the florid mantle which capped the hunched shoulders.

Hugh's eyes narrowed. "You must let me correspond with my parents," he demanded. "No harm can come of that."

"I am not here to do your bidding, Master O'Donnell," Perrot snapped, and then tapered off to the same pleasant tone. "You Irish are clever and I've no doubt but that you could devise a code which would cause my officers no end of worry. No, sir, I think not. You shall remain here in the custody of no one but my trusted servants. You shall have every freedom that we can allow. Oh, we do not expect that you will be a model prisoner but we are prepared for any plans you may have to leave us. If you attempt this we shall revoke your privileges and clap you in irons where you will stay and rot." He paused before he continued in the same even temper. "Your parents will be informed that you are here and well. And we shall represent this whole affair as rather tragic but inevitable. Even Master Dudall shall be disciplined so that the proper forms are observed."

"You'd punish one of your own men?" Hugh asked in disbelief.

Perrot nodded. "Oh, indeed. This is a perilous business, this court intrigue, this political existence. We are but hours compared to numberless days and one leaves to make way for the next. We—" But there was no more to say so he shrugged and motioned for the guards to lead the boy away. "The interview is at an end. Good day, sir." He went back to his papers, his bald head lost in other thoughts.

Hugh was ushered to his chamber in the famed Birmingham Tower of the castle—a thick, black cylinder of ugly masonry which faced the southeast. For a prison cell it was not as bad as the boy had imagined. In fact, it resembled the living quarters of many a merchant Irishman whose trade had raised him above the level of the peasant. The interior had a small carpet set over the flagstone floor and the walls were simply but attractively outlined in dark paneled frames. The ceiling was low, supported by two large crossbeams and several interlacing timbers. A fireplace was cut into one wall of the room and a plain wooden cot stood clumsily against the opposite wall. Rounding out the furniture was a squat, unfinished stool and a badly defaced table. The only light came from a high, barred window which faced west in a direction parallel to the river. Hugh, now free of his chains, stood in the center of the room and scarcely noticed that the jailer had left, shut the door, and shot the locking bar into place.

Hugh lost little time before examining his prison. He went first to the window and found it necessary to stand on the stool in order to look out. The bars were set well apart and Hugh guessed that he could just squeeze through them. But what then? Some hundred feet below yawned the moat, its banks constantly patrolled by the English foot soldiers. Above was the summit of the tower where sentries kept their steady watch throughout the day and night. Even now Hugh could hear the measured tread of a pikeman overhead. Twisting his body around, he thrust his head between the bars and looked up. One of the sentries looked down at the same instant and arched his eyebrows as if to say, "Not this way, my friend!"

Next Hugh tried the fireplace but saw that the chimney narrowed so that the passage of a body would be impossible. An iron bar cut across the chimney part way up to further obstruct movement. He tested the door and walls and found them all stout and well made. "There must be a way out!" he told himself between clenched teeth. But no way seemed to offer itself and Hugh finally lay down on his cot and listened to the monotonous tromp of the English boots above. His own young heart matched each step and the harmony eventually sent him into a deep sleep.

In the morning he began his first day of prison routine. His breakfast—some oat cakes and sour cream—was brought to him by a grinning hunchback and two armed guards. All meals were thus delivered to him and the leftover dishes were retrieved in the same manner. Some books were allowed him, many with an eye to converting him to the English way of life and very few for the purpose of enjoyment. Teachers were provided on occasion and they outlined for him the history they would have him believe. He was told that the Irish were barbarians, that they were slaves to a foreign pope, that the Spaniards would desert them as allies. Every manner of half-truth and absolute lie was manufactured. Hugh asked many questions and the tutors thought him an excellent pupil. But the prince was biding his time.

He was permitted to read some historical accounts

of the great generals and great battles of the past and he thus further steeped himself in military lore. He learned how the enemy equipped itself in battle and he committed to memory the tactics they employed. Often he created battle problems within the confines of his own cell and solved them with paper armies and penciled plans. "How like my poor father," he thought, "with his crude, crumpled relics." His exemplary conduct was rewarded by the use of writing paper but none was ever to pass from his cell.

Perrot visited him on occasion. "May I have a priest come to see me?" Hugh begged him, "just to hear my confession and perhaps say Mass of a time?"

The viceroy shook his head slowly, as if the decision were pleasantly painful. "Oh no, my boy, there'll be none of that. These priests I trust least of all and it's not likely I'd allow them—in their black garments and strange tongue—to disarrange the fine job my servants have done with you. No, no! None of that! Do not ask again."

It was Hugh's sentence that he should speak to no one but the English guards. He sometimes played at chess or other games with them but very little friendly conversation was exchanged. The guards had been warned that Hugh was a fanatic and they were not to trust him. In spite of this, a number of them came to hold the fearless, dauntless boy in their respect. These few would sometimes bring him news from the North or smuggle him books he desired to read. Once, through a sentry, he was able to deliver a message to his parents telling them not to worry, that he still lived. More than this the friendly guards dared not do, however, for there were many among their companions who hated the red-haired lad and would report any favorable action toward him.

Hugh did not give up the hope of escaping. He studied the prison habits, the changing of the guards, the layout of the castle as he heard it from others, the confines of his own cell. He set all of these facts down against the day when he could put his plan into operation. One of the big stumbling blocks, next to the castle itself, was the fact that he was not familiar with Dublin and the neighboring country. He might work out a successful exit from the jail only to be recaptured again within the Pale.

But he continued to scheme. Those who passed by were used to seeing the lone figure peering from the cell window at the far reaches of the River Liffey or looking sadly down at the normal life of Dublin which paraded before him. Even the fierce snows of winter or the driving spring rains failed to keep him from his daily vigil. The boy who had freely roamed the North country—riding, fishing, hunting, and fighting at his leisure—could not accustom himself to his present restraint. He chafed at the confinement and bent all of his efforts toward effecting his own release. But he did so silently, behaving outwardly as one in complete submission to English authority.

Just as silently as the prisoner served, so did the seasons change. Each made its singular impression on the life and architecture of the castle. Fall was the most pleasant with its crisp, clean air and its stimulus to activity. Then came winter whose white presence wrapped the dreary dungeon in once-a-year splendor but brought with it a chilling numbness to its inhabitants. The moat and the castle stream were swollen under the assault of the spring rains and then followed summer with the blistering heat which crept into every cell until the barred windows were as smoldering brands to the touch.

A curious rat or mouse sometimes wandered into Hugh's high chamber. Once he nursed to health and freedom a crippled bird that had wisely collapsed on his cell window. Outside the pattern of life was always changing. New ships called on the port. New homes took shape and new citizens moved in to occupy them. But, from Birmingham Tower, Hugh witnessed no internal change. The same guards, the same bleak landscape, and the same wry and resolute commander filled the scene.

Thoughts of home were painful and he tried to keep from dwelling on the soft black locks of Kathleen or from fearing for his parents in the critical province of Donegal. When his fantasies would reach their most absurd proportions he thought that MacSweeney with his ax-bearing infantry might rescue him. But saner moments told him that MacSweeney and his friends in the North had problems of their own to meet. Nor did he doubt but that the English watched their every move. If he were to escape, it would have to be through a method of his own devising.

In this way three years passed for Red Hugh O'Donnell. The Spanish Armada had been shattered by British sea power and the fury of the Atlantic. The English sea dogs were sailing on to the discovery of new countries and new treasures. O'Neill was skirmishing with Elizabeth's soldiers and all Ireland lay as a dry leaf near a low candle. Three long years! The candle burned for Hugh, too, and it was a slow flame searing him but enlightening him as well. It was a spark rapidly becoming a conflagration—a blaze that would one day crackle at the very doorstep of the English sovereign.

chapter 8

DURING THE three years of his confinement, Hugh had won some special privileges for himself. He was now permitted some closely guarded exercise in the courtyard and, on occasion, a visit with a few select fellow prisoners. These meetings were brief and always attended by English soldiers. Still they served as a welcome relief from the monotony of the imprisonment and they gave him an opportunity to preserve his physical well-being.

Sometimes, in the courtyard, Hugh would clash with a comrade in a battle of wooden swords. These encounters were always cheered by the garrison but no Englishman ever joined the combatants. The guards were usually content to admire from afar and applaud the strength displayed when the game turned to wrestling and the young Irishmen tumbled about the square until everyone expected a skull to be fractured. But only aches and pains seemed to be the result and Hugh had a few of these, though he managed to best all of the prisoners that came against him.

One warm afternoon Hugh had just disposed of another challenger and was leaving the arena with his arm about his adversary when a voice stopped him.

"You there. You with the red hair!"

Hugh turned to see one of the officers, a brute of a man who was known as Captain Leeds, striding across the yard after him. This big man with the coarse features and unruly hair studied Hugh momentarily when he had reached his side.

Then he grinned at the boy maliciously. "So you think you have some skill with those arms of yours? That's because you have not met me. I'm not one of your soft Irish friends. Would you care to try a fall with Leeds—with me?"

The prince was about to refuse but the captain had already removed his shirt and stood waiting with his legs spread apart. Hugh shrugged, drew a deep breath, and moved in on the Englishman. Leeds was a powerful man and he seemed to tower over Hugh as MacSweeney had done. When Hugh reached out to take him by the arm the officer lunged forward and smashed him in the face with his head. Hugh went down with blood streaming from his nose and his eyes blurred out of focus. He had no chance to recover. Leeds kicked him in the side and then dropped on his stomach with his knees. The breath escaped from Hugh in a pitiful moan.

Mutterings of displeasure arose from some of the English soldiers watching, but they dared not interfere and they prevented the Irish prisoners from offering assistance.

The captain dragged Hugh to his feet and, lifting him above his head in his massive arms, hurled him to the earth. Hugh felt himself go limp and he watched the nailed boot again drive at his side. Suddenly he rolled over and caught Leeds' foot with his own and brought the officer to earth. Acting almost on reflex now, he swung on top of his opponent and reached for his throat. He knew he had not the strength to thus end the encounter but he hoped to manage the bully until he had regained a little of his own composure. Leeds suddenly thrust Hugh's arms apart and spun him upward with a blow from his knee.

Hugh was on his feet now, bleeding and covered with dust, but he was alert and ready for the new attack. The two men circled each other looking for an opening. Abruptly the captain lashed out with his fist and caught Hugh high on the temple. Hugh recoiled and the officer followed his advantage with a blow that slid off Hugh's shoulder. Hugh ducked another savage punch and struck Leeds in the stomach with all the force at his command. The big man doubled up for a moment and Hugh was on him punishing him with blows to the head that sent him reeling against the garrison hitching rack. A solid smash flush in the face of the giant catapulted him over the rail and he landed with a thud in the dust, his feet still hooked on the crossbar. The prince swung under the bar, kicked the captain free, and rolled him on his stomach. Then he sat astride Leeds and, twisting his huge arm backward in a painful arc, called upon that officer to surrender. The man bellowed, "Guards!" and Hugh was dragged from the miserable form.

When Leeds staggered to his feet he made as if to strike Hugh who was now pinioned in the arms of two soldiers but these men looked so hard at their captain that he hobbled off, cursing, and without obeying his impulse. The guards released Hugh who then sank to the ground, closed his eyes in pain and fatigue, and pushed his hand against his throbbing nose to stem the bleeding. Art Kavanagh came to his assistance with a wet cloth and propped Hugh up with his arms.

Art, somewhat older than Hugh, was here as the result of an unsuccessful raid on an English ammunition train that once passed through his native Wexford. He had paid for his daring. The tendons of his legs had been cut and his movements were agony. But he shuffled over to Hugh and bathed his wound.

"Well, now," Art said, "that was a fine piece of business. You've made yourself a dear friend there, I'm sure."

"It was him that started it," Hugh protested between gasps. "I'd no mind for it myself 'til he fell upon me and beat me, he did."

"Ah, yes, yes. It's not blaming you I am. Just warning you."

Hugh felt better now and drew a clean breath. He got to his feet with the help of his fellow prisoner.

"Thank you, Art, for the assistance and the warning. But I'll not be staying here much longer if I have my way."

"You've a plan then?"

"Aye, the nibblin' of one, but I've not yet resolved what I'll do surely when once I'm outside."

Art smiled and said, "Well, now, and if that's your problem, you've come to the right man. I know every foot of this woeful town and it's glad I'd be to map it for you since I'll not be leavin' myself."

"I'll gladly take you with me."

Art shook his head sadly. "It's not far you'd be getting with me along. Not past the first gate, I'd warrant. No lad, I'll help, but I can't go with you. Tomorrow when we meet I'll deliver the map to you. It'll be from memory"—he tapped his head—"but it's as good as the queen's compass."

An archer from a nearby tower called down, "Hey there! Move on in!"

Hugh and Art parted with a wink and the prince felt, for the first time in months, a new determination and courage well up in him in spite of the aches and pains.

True to his word, Art Kavanagh met with Hugh the following morning and entered into conversation with him.

"Here's some news to gladden your ears, Hugh lad. They do say that Captain Leeds has been reprimanded by the commandant for his little fight with you. I expect he'll like you no more for that favor."

Hugh shrugged. One could be sure of very little here. Perrot had deported Dudall to England to cover his own scheming and now it was heard in the castle that Dudall had the queen's ear and was turning her against the viceroy. One lived with the present and that's why Hugh sighed. "Do you have the map?"

"Of course. Would I come without it now? It is here." And Art slipped a folded sheet to Hugh.

"I'm grateful to you, that's sure, and I'll have the monks of Donegal remember you when I arrive home."

"When do you plan to make this attempt?"

"I can't give you the details now." Hugh bent to lace his boot. One of the guards had moved toward them to interrupt their conversation.

Hugh added quickly, "On the first stormy evening from this day, I shall be over the wall and into the streets of Dublin."

"Head south for the Wicklow Mountains," Art advised him. "It's close and O'Toole's friendly there."

Hugh thanked his friend with a nod as the sentry came abreast of them and prodded them apart with his pike. As he motioned them back to their quarters, Art glanced at Hugh.

"I do hope it will rain soon," he said. "The good Lord knows the darlin' farmers do be needin' every drop of it."

The English soldier shouted at them and they returned to their cells.

As it developed, it was none too soon that Kavanagh had provided the map. For the kind comrade was taken ill shortly thereafter and confined to his bed for an indefinite period. Hugh committed the paper to memory and burned it.

It was more than two weeks before any rain fell. But when it did come it came in torrents. The thunder rolled across the heavens like the chariot of Cuchullain and flashes of lightning illuminated the city streets and the grim walls of the castle. Inside Birmingham Tower, Hugh was already at work.

He had noticed that the archers left the tower summit on stormy days and waited out the rain in the guard room. That left but one guard in the passageway and he was slouched against a door at the far end of the long hall. In that position he was unable to hear any noise from Hugh's chamber. And a good thing this was, for Hugh was currently engaged in a very loud undertaking.

Bracing himself against the sides of the chimney, he inched up to the iron bar which cut across the opening and began chipping away at the extremities of it with a jagged piece of iron. It was tiresome work and Hugh had to descend to his room frequently to check on the movements of the guard and to rest. After nearly an hour of work, he had loosened the rod somewhat and now he relaxed his brace on the chimney's sides and swung his full weight on the bar. The remaining masonry crumbled and Hugh, bar and all, came tumbling down into the fireplace.

The prince smiled to himself and lightly waved the thick shaft. Now he had both a tool and a weapon and he set about using it. Dragging the stool to the center of the floor, he sought a panel in the ceiling which he had marked as lying directly beneath the platform above. He commenced to pry and hammer on this until the wood gave way. He repeated the process on the flagstones which he next encountered. This proved more difficult but the heavy bar seemed to work wonders in his eager hands. In a short time he had broken through the summit of the tower. He drew himself up by his hands to the rain-soaked roof and gave a quick look around. No one was in sight. He then dropped back to his room, gathered his few belongings and the makeshift crowbar and threw them up ahead of him. Then he clambered through the opening into the storm-tossed twilight. The wild cloud-burst ran off his clothes in dirty little streams and washed the soot from his body.

Hugh crept down the stair to the guard room. The door was ajar and he could see three or four soldiers seated at a table playing cards. Another two or three were sleeping. He slipped noiselessly toward the door but, at that instant, one of the Englishmen looked up and saw him. The guard was on his feet with a cry of alarm on his lips. But Hugh was quicker. He dashed to the door and threw the heavy bolt which secured it from without. The trapped guards pounded on the door with the hilts of their swords but most of the din was lost in the fury of the tempest outside. Enough of it reached the remaining sentry, however, to bring him running from his gallery post.

The young O'Donnell heard him coming and waited for him in the shadow of a broad stone pillar, his crowbar poised. The guardsman walked rapidly past with drawn sword and caught only a fleeting glimpse of movement as the iron bar crashed against the back of his helmeted skull. Hugh stepped to the man's unconscious body and relieved him of his short sword and small pistol. His next thoughts were of the prisoners in other parts of the castle but he was unfamiliar with their location and the position of their guards, so he gave up the idea and started off alone.

The pounding of the tower guards faded as Hugh moved silently along the deserted hallway which led to the open courtyard. He crossed the slimy yard where the mud oozed under the impress of his boots. Keeping within the dark screen of the buildings, he maintained a watchful eye for any movement from the garrison. From the main room of the castle a little light leaked out and Hugh could discern the figure of Perrot bent over some papers. If Sir John only knew what was taking place but a few short yards from him, his evening labors would have been much less tranquil.

Suddenly Hugh stopped. A raincoated soldier swinging a lantern was moving across the square toward him. Hugh cocked his pistol.

"Who's there?" the Englishman called.

Hugh said a little silent prayer and then came forth with what he hoped was a fair imitation of the English accent his ears had been accustomed to these many years.

"It's only a cook, sir," he said, "bringing some tea to the guards."

There was a moment of silence before the soldier called back. "Very well. Be off then. Lord knows the lads could use a cup on a fearsome night like this." Then the lantern and its owner slowly disappeared into the storm.

Hugh moved quickly to a corner of the yard where the wall joined a small chapel. Here the window ledges afforded a grip for the hands and feet and, with their assistance, he managed to gain the top of the wall. It was a fair drop to the rain-filled ditch but he knew he must take the risk. Normally the moat would have been filled but the attendants had drained it two days before and left a coating of slime further aggravated by the violent rain. Taking a deep breath, Hugh stepped out into the darkness. As he leaped, his jacket caught on a projecting stone and jolted him back against the wall. Then the fabric ripped and he plunged into the soggy moat. His right leg twisted under him and he cried out a little in pain. After he had managed to scramble up the slippery embankment and had reached the road, he felt the sharp stab of the injured leg, but he set his teeth and limped off into the night.

He groped his way southward through the city in

order to make for the nearest friendly shelter—the mountains of Wicklow. The rains continued their steady downpour but the thunder and lightning abated. A few acres of blackened sky growled in retreat. Thoroughly drenched, Hugh prayed that the storm would continue so that his departure would go unnoticed that much longer.

Through the moist streets he made his way, pausing now and then to check on any pursuit and then sallying forth once more toward the south with as much speed as the pain in his leg would allow. He saw hardly a soul on his way and those he did meet were too interested in keeping dry to notice him. At last he reached the southern gate of the town and found it not only open but unguarded. He passed through and then huddled against the outside wall to rest. He licked the salt water from his lips and threw his head back to enjoy a moment of careless oblivion. Then on again into the dreary evening where the glossy fields spread out before him.

Safety lay a scant fifteen or twenty miles away in Wicklow and from there Hugh had hopes of swinging west and then north into Donegal. The storm buffeted him as he trekked steadily southward toward Featherbed Pass. For a mile or so he followed the course of the Dodder River, then crossed it where its banks narrowed and swept on through pine forests and past the legendary Glen of the Thrushes.

Hugh's leg continued to trouble him and every step was a new experience in pain. He felt certain that his escape had been discovered by now and imagined that a search party was already forming. He thought of Perrot who would be disturbed in his cold, grim way and he thought of Art Kavanagh who he knew was pulling for him to make good the break. The English would be mounted and could easily close the few miles he had put between himself and Dublin. This realization lent a crippled version of speed to his flight.

At length he found himself at the foot of Three Rock Mountain, its stubby, rain-washed trees drooping like wet fleece, and he stumbled across this landmark pulling himself from shrub to shrub with his bruised hands. He dragged himself up the slope, tearing his garments in the ascent. The rain began to slacken and finally died completely. Little rivulets ran down the sides of the hills and theirs was the only sound in the bleak night save his own heavy breathing and quickening step.

From Three Rock Mountain Hugh looked down on Glencree, a valley of rugged beauty which curved for nearly ten miles from the base of the Great Sugar Loaf to the foot of the Glendoo Mountain. On both sides granite boulders were strewn about in wild confusion as a mute reminder of the age of glaciers and the tiny Glencree River darted through the rocky defile. Once through Glencree, the flight would be relatively safe since the mountain fastness of Wicklow contained many clans whose chiefs were hostile to the English. A hiding place was virtually assured and Hugh was cheered by the prospect.

But, at that moment, he slipped on a loose bit of rock and crumbled to the wet earth. Exhaustion was like a rope, tight about his chest, and he had no power to rise. Three years in a dungeon had cramped his limbs and the unfortunate fall had further impaired his ability to travel. He was no longer the Hugh that bounded like a deer on the slopes of Croaghan. His feet were torn and bleeding, and his strength was gone.

"I'll rest here just a little while," he told himself, "and then I'll go on."

He edged over to a sheltering cliff and swept the pine-covered floor of the valley with his gaze before lying back to rest. The sky was now blown clear of its clouds and the heaving moon sprayed light on the sides of the ridge and made them glisten. He could not sleep for the pain but braced himself against the overhanging rock and kept his eyes riveted on the roadway below. He knew there would be riders along that path before long. The English, perhaps, or even one of O'Toole's patrols. He would have to wait and see. All thought of further flight had disappeared and he sat in the lap of the inevitable.

The dampness of his clothes reached him and he shivered. With his weary hands he chafed his arms and legs but made no attempt to rise. The hours slipped by and the dark sky ebbed to gray. Dawn would bring new problems, for a daylight journey would be much more difficult. With growing impatience, he waited for a sign of help.

Then he caught the regular hoofbeats of horses moving along the mud-soaked highway. He listened with a hand upon his pistol.

chapter 9

PAINFULLY HUGH raised himself and propped his trembling back against the wall of rock. He peered into the budding morning and was now able to discern three horsemen moving rapidly down the road. This was too small a party to be pursuing a fugitive. The trio had to be Irish and their greeting in Gaelic when they spied him dispelled all doubt.

It was Phelim O'Toole himself and two of his officers. O'Toole was one of the chieftains who roamed the Wicklow Mountains making both a home and a fortress of them. Stout is what you might call him, with rosy cheeks and a paunch that was draped over the gold belt he wore. But he was a warrior as fine as any in the South providing the encounter did not last too long. And Phelim O'Toole usually saw that it didn't!

With some difficulty the horsemen scaled the peak and reached Hugh's resting place. Looking for all the world like an obese little elf, the Wicklow chieftain dismounted and shook Hugh's hand vigorously. Hugh smiled at the comic figure, but his joy at seeing a countryman built up to laughter.

O'Toole chuckled, too. "Hardly a night for a walk," he said. "You should have told me you planned to call."

"The walk was not my idea, I assure you," said Hugh, "but when one is in such poor straits, one cannot choose. To whom do I owe this timely deliverance?"

The chieftain patted himself on his sloping chest. "Why, 'tis O'Toole you're talking to, lad. Phelim O'Toole of Glendalough. And unless I be mistaken, this would be the young Hugh Roe O'Donnell of Donegal."

Hugh was surprised. "You know me?"

"Let us say your fame has traveled before you. Had Sir John Perrot the same sources of information as I, you'd have been back in his hands hours ago. My men and I have been scouring the area looking for you."

"I thank you, sir," Hugh said. "My father will reward you for this."

O'Toole shushed him. "Och, talk not of rewards, my boy. It's glad I am to do a little for me country—and, I might add, to do a little against another country we won't mention. C'mon now, mount up behind me."

The three horses breathed heavily under the two silent officers and their volatile leader and their breath threw a faint mist upon the scene. Hugh reached for the saddle cantle to hoist himself up when he was stopped by the firm hand of O'Toole upon his shoulder.

"Listen!"

To the north they heard the hoofbeats of horses at full speed and knew then that the English were on the road. In the full glare of daylight which was now upon them they could see an entire group of cavalry splashing down the mountain highway. At the same moment, the leader of the horsemen spotted them and cut off the road in pursuit.

O'Toole, with a quick glance at the enemy, swung Hugh up behind him and turned toward the valley of Glencree. But, before they had as much as put a spur to their mounts, they saw another section of cavalry streaming out across the valley floor from the eastern side of Two Rock Mountain. They were hemmed in! Already some of the English had dismounted and had begun to ascend the hill on foot, their short bows unlimbered and ready.

The old chieftain turned sadly to the weary boy. "I'm afraid the game is up," he said. "We are outnumbered and cannot break through their lines."

Hugh sighed with resignation. "I am sorry for you, sir, sorry as the tears of Erin, that I brought you to this."

The pursuers drew closer and the Irishmen waited with muffled impatience.

"Perhaps all is not lost," O'Toole offered. "If I am jailed I cannot help you but if I remain free I may be of some future assistance. They'll be here in a few moments, so listen carefully. We shall ride down to meet them and I'll turn you over to them as an escaped prisoner. This is a poor solution, but the only one that comes to my ancient mind."

Hugh did not argue. He nodded his agreement and the small party clambered down the slope to meet the main body of cavalry. Their descent was covered by English archers but, at the command of their captain, they held their fire. The instant the prince heard the voice he knew it was Captain Leeds who had trapped them on the mountain.

At a slow walk, the Irish approached the unit commander. O'Toole saluted and addressed him courteously. "Phelim O'Toole at your honor's service. Returning an escaped prisoner. I trust there is a suitable reward."

Leeds eyed him suspiciously and remarked, "When we came upon you, you seemed to be turning south. Dublin, you know, is north."

O'Toole threw up his hands and put on his most engaging smile. "A small error on our part," he said. "We spotted the horsemen in Glencree and thought we'd ride down to join them. Had we seen your worship in time, why, to be sure, we'd have turned north."

"Hm," the cavalry leader mused. "You Irish are as ready with your tongues as you are with your swords. But it is no matter. We have our prisoner and you are of no value to us—though I should string you up from the nearest limb . . . if there were a tree large enough to hold your bulk."

O'Toole bowed in mock submission and Leeds

waved him aside. "Disarm the boy and bring him to me," he commanded. "And be not too gentle about it."

The soldiers dragged Hugh cruelly from the saddle, stripped off his sword and pistol, and set him before the captain. The savage face of his tormentor was like another ache upon his tortured body.

Leeds nodded wryly. "A little journey you had in mind, eh, Master O'Donnell? A little adventure, perhaps?"

Hugh closed his eyes and remained silent. The angered captain struck him across the face with his heavy mailed glove and spun him to the soggy turf. Hugh started to rise but slipped back again with his arms reaching out toward Glencree. O'Toole bit his plump lip but dared not move or it would have spelled death for all of them.

Leeds stared for a moment at the prisoner and then called, "Lieutenant Simms, take part of the troop and make sure this area is clear of the barbarians. Sergeant, throw this wretch on a horse and follow me."

A large section of the cavalry unit wheeled about and galloped north again with Hugh's body sprawled inert across the shoulders of a large black mare. In this fashion they return to Dublin and their entry into the city was cheered by the partisan crowd, many of whom were elated to witness the miserable state of the fugitive. "May his blood run as red as his hair," one jeered and a little boy spit at him. Hugh had left his last friends at the side of Two Rock Mountain when O'Toole rode dejectedly away to the south. He felt himself being swallowed again in the dark waters of the Dublin pool.

At length the detachment ambled into the castle. A limp burden upon the indifferent animal, Hugh was jogged back to consciousness and gazed through unsteady eyes at the familiar landmarks—the massive bridge, the black moat, the ashen wall, and, finally, the forbidding tower which had been his residence for more than three years. In all this time he could point to but one short, ill-fated day of freedom.

The unit stopped in the courtyard and Hugh was dumped unceremoniously to the ground. The captain prodded him roughly with his boot and ordered him to stand.

Hugh's leg burned with pain as he felt for the stirrup of the mare and hauled himself up. His lip bled from the impress of his clenched teeth and the aching leg shocked his features into a twisted grimace. He held to the saddle horn in order to stay erect. Then he saw Sir John Perrot approaching slowly like a housewife surveying a disagreeable task.

The Viceroy fixed him with a cold stare which showed neither pity nor anger. When he spoke at last it was as before—carefully and slowly.

"I see that good advice does not set well with you," he said. "You have caused us a great loss of sleep and have put my men to a severe inconvenience. You were warned of the consequences. From this hour forth you will be secured with irons and you will be treated as the lowest criminal is treated in the prison houses of Spain. I warrant you will find another escape quite impossible." He turned on his heel and left.

Hugh was dragged once more to Birmingham Tower and escorted to the familiar cell. While he watched, clamps were driven into the base of the fireplace and the fixture was then cemented over. He fell into a sound sleep, under guard, as the substance hardened and woke to find a length of chain fastened to the twin clamps and its extremities firmly bound to his ankles. The shackles permitted him to move awkwardly about the room but were so designed that he could not reach the window or the newly patched ceiling.

For several weeks the prison doctor visited him and applied heat and ointment to his injured leg. Soon it was healed and its scar was more mental than physical. Nor was the doctor the only visitor. When a week or two had passed following the capture, Leeds entered the chamber.

Hugh returned the hatred the captain apparently felt toward him. For both men the other seemed to be a symbol of all they detested in the other's nationality. Hugh stood grudgingly when the Englishman entered, and Leeds seated himself leaving Hugh standing without explanation. There was some secret thought deep in his animal brain and Hugh wished with all his heart he could wrench it forth.

"Sit down!" the captain shouted, driving Hugh against the fireplace with his heavy boot. His feet tangled in the chains, Hugh sank ponderously to the stone floor. Leeds rose and bent over him. The lack of fear revealed in Hugh's eyes annoyed Leeds and he brought his hand down viciously across Hugh's mouth.

"I'll teach you respect," he screamed. "I'll teach you what fear means! Get used to it. You'll see more of me. A lot more than you would care to see. I'll make you crawl for a corner each time I enter your cell."

Hugh answered him evenly. "If it's after frightening me you are, Mister Leeds, sure now, you can save your precious breath. I'll not let that happen though you beat me worse than a flail the wheat. And I think, too, saving your humble presence, that Sir John Perrot would not care to see his prisoner abused in such a fashion."

The captain interrupted him with a roar of laughter. "Sir John Perrot, is it? The devil take him! I guess you didn't hear there's a new viceroy come to join us—Sir William Fitzwilliam. Arrived today from London where your old friend, Sir John, is now bound."

"It was Dudall caused his downfall or I'm a sinner," Hugh said.

"Aye," Leeds replied with another throaty laugh, "the same. A measly man that, but he done me a good turn. Our new master says I'm in charge of this section of the prison and he's none too interested in how I perform my duties."

"We'll get along, I'm sure," said Hugh sarcastically.

"Aye, I'm sure." Leeds rose and kicked over Hugh's small cask of water. "Now you wasn't thirsty anyway, was you, Master O'Donnell? The rain must have soaked you so two weeks ago that you'll not be needing much at all to drink. I'll tell the warden to cut your ration. And I'll be back. I can promise you that." He slammed the grate behind him.

Hugh never laid eyes on Fitzwilliam and, for all he knew, the prison force might have been composed only of the cruel Leeds and the few guards that stationed themselves in relays outside his chamber door. The new viceroy was a weak man, given to drink and fits of illness, and content to leave the management of the castle to Leeds and the other captains. Hugh's self-appointed torturer plagued him at every turn—with physical punishment from his clublike fists, with threats and taunts, with restrictions on food and water. In spite of this, Hugh refused to buckle and kept up an inflexible exterior. But his failure to escape and the new restraints placed upon him had sapped his hopes and were feeding on the limits of his courage. Deliverance seemed further from his grasp than ever before. His frequent fits of despair had none of the welcome relief formerly furnished by the strolls about the courtyard and the brief talks he enjoyed with fellow inmates. He could not even reach the window so that he might see Art Kavanagh and the others who shared this existence with him. Books and other pleasures were forfeit and his days consisted of endless hours of sleep and futile thought. Even the brutal interviews of the captain provided a stimulus that snapped the monotony. No other voice greeted him. The once-friendly jailers kept a timid silence and only the sounds of alien conversation, all about him and never to him, reached him as if he were an audience from another world.

Winter and spring passed in this fashion and the summer months, scorching the landscape from July to September, found him more desperate than ever. Escape once again became his prime concern, more now for the sake of his sanity than for the freedom itself. There was little hope of rescue now and still less of a chance that the English would relent and release him. Yet every plan that presented itself seemed impossible of completion. The wary guards kept him under constant surveillance and the weight of the chains seemed to increase day by day. Should he successfully hurdle these obstacles there was the castle itself to consider and the difficult trek to Wicklow where he had failed once before.

The oppressive heat seemed to kindle the stones of his foul dungeon and cauterize every happy memory of the North country. Even the vision of his grieving parents and of the lovely Kathleen struggled in the dimness of his doubt. He was nearing the age of twenty and the prospect of spending his life in

this selfsame cell loomed as probable. He ate list-
lessly and gave up the few limited exercises he had
been doing to keep his body strong. The clank of his
chain on the floor resounded dully as if no living
thing inhabited the chamber. He had reached the
depths.

September found him, one night, stretched upon
his cot, his arm across his eyes. The patch of sky he
could see flashed its private stars at him through the
ribs of the window and a cool breeze settled effort-
lessly on his gaunt face. The harsh noises of Dublin
assailed his ears for a time and were then replaced by
the sweet song of some wandering minstrel. The melody was strange and sad, and yet somehow familiar.

Hugh sat straight up on his bed. He knew that
voice! It was Martin of Cloghan!

chapteR 10

HUGH SWUNG his body from the hard cot and hobbled the length of the fetters so that he might hear better.

"What is Martin doing here?" he wondered aloud. If he could only see him and speak to him a moment of his parents and Kathleen and the Donegal that he loved. He considered crying out to the man but stilled the impulse in order to drink in the words of the North country ballad. Hugh heard him sing all the songs he loved in his youth—"The Fairy Maid," "The Boast of Brian Boru," "The Piper of the Glen," and countless others.

Below he could hear the voices of the English soldiers calling for more music and for an hour or more Martin entertained them. And he delighted, too, the young prince he had served so long and was now planning to serve again.

After a long time, the serenade seemed to decline and die away altogether. Soon the courtyard was hushed. Only the call of the watch naming the hour of midnight stabbed at the silence. Hugh was sunk in reverie and had begun to wonder whether it was indeed the voice of Martin he had heard. Or was this the beginning of the insanity he feared so much? Was the melody a fantastic creation of his own groping mind? The conjecture was soon shattered by the whirr of an arrow which split the window, glanced off the ceiling, and fell a few feet from the prisoner. A slip of parchment trailed from the shaft and Hugh hurriedly plucked it off and read it.

"Burn the arrow and the note when you have read the message," it began. "Your parents send greetings. They are well but worry about you. Do not despair. Soon you shall be with them again. Henry and Art O'Neill, son of the chieftain O'Neill, are prisoners here in Dublin Castle. I am to help the three of you escape but it will take some time. A man must be selected, bought, and then a plan woven about him. Keep your courage and be ready for any eventuality. God's wisdom to guide you and His hand to guard you."

For the first time in months the prince smiled. He crumpled the paper in his quivering hand and held it as a man would scoop and treasure a pinch of dirt from his homeland. Then he kicked the broken arrow into the fireplace and cast the note after it. Fortunately the day had been chilly and a small fire burned in his room. Soon a thin trail of smoke was all that remained of the incident.

In another room of the castle the sons of O'Neill were plotting on their own. Like Hugh they had been taken as hostages against an uprising in the North but their treatment at the hands of the English had been less severe. Art and Henry had pretended to accept the indoctrination of their English tutors and they were permitted to stroll, almost at leisure, about the fortress. Their journey this day brought them together with Martin and they learned of the scheme to free them. Martin was to take up residence in Dublin and would furnish part of the gold needed for the bribe. Then he would see to it that horses were provided for the fugitives and he would lead them out of the city. It would be left to the O'Neills to discover the means for the escape and the method whereby Hugh O'Donnell could accompany them.

Henry O'Neill, though the younger of the two brothers, was a natural leader, like Red Hugh himself, and he studied his captors, trying to determine which one of them could be tempted. It took him two weeks to pick his man, a thin, squinting fellow whose jaws worked nervously as he listened to the plans of the brothers.

When he heard them out he pleaded, "All of those ideas are too rash. One misstep would mean my life and yours as well. We must be patient. These things take time."

"What about O'Donnell?" Henry asked.

The guard shook his head. "That is another problem. You will be better off going it alone. O'Donnell is chained and closely watched. Freeing him would be a risky business."

"We'll take the risk," Henry answered him sharply.

"It will take more money," the guard advised him.

"That, too, you'll have," Art promised. "But we won't leave without Red Hugh, so set your greedy mind to thinking."

The guard shook his head doubtfully, the veins standing out curiously on his temples. "You are fools. But I shall try. No amount of money in the world will help me if I'm caught."

"Now, then," Henry reminded him, "that's your problem. You will be paid well for your services. Now be off and come to us next with a plan of your own invention."

Meanwhile, Hugh, ignorant of the moves being made to assist him, lived on in renewed hope. The dawns he had given up noticing now warmed him with the promise of freedom. His meals held more interest for him and he resumed the exercises he had abandoned months before.

Delay followed delay, however. The guard was frightened and his fear led to weeks of inactivity. Then Art O'Neill became ill and took to his bed. It was a long illness which ran its feverish course through September and October. The disease swept through the prison and took the life of Art Kavanagh and a number of Irish inmates who were too weak to resist. Hugh and Henry were spared and Art O'Neill finally began to recover, but very slowly. Nevertheless, he urged Henry to proceed with his plans for the escape.

The lean fall days gave way quickly to winter and Dublin shivered in the cold grip of December when their accomplice paid the O'Neills a surprise visit.

"I have arranged everything," he told them, "for the eve of the Epiphany, a few weeks from this date. On that day a special celebration will be held at the castle to which the veteran guards have been invited. I, being one of the newcomers, have drawn the Tower watch."

"And what of Hugh O'Donnell?"

"He shall come, too, as you wished. I shall have the keys to his cell but the manacles present a problem."

"Can we not slip him a file before that time, together with a note informing him of our plans?"

"It would be most dangerous."

"The entire venture is dangerous. Bring him the file at your earliest opportunity and you shall be repaid."

"Ah, yes, that is another question." The squint-eyed one looked warily from one O'Neill to the other. "When do my masters plan to fulfill this contract?"

"When we are clear of the English and safe in our homeland."

"No, no! I do not go that far."

Henry laughed at the guard.

"Surely, you did not plan to stay here after our escape? You'd be hung as a traitor."

The warder shuddered. "That is true, but my life

would be in as grave danger in your country. You must think of something else."

"Very well," said Art. "Henry and I shall see that payment is made when we contact O'Toole or O'Byrne in Wicklow. Then our father will repay him when we reach Tyrone in the North."

The proposal met with the approval of the Englishman and the three set about making careful preparations for the flight. A small quantity of food could certainly be secured by Martin but the more immediate needs called for a rope, weapons, and some horses. The accomplice was instructed to contact the waiting shanachie and to inform him of their requirements. Martin assured him that the horses would be waiting in the street next to the Birmingham Tower and supplied the guard with a brace of pistols. The rope and any other side arms would be the Englishman's charge.

At about the same time the entire plan was made known to Hugh and a file was slipped to him during the hubbub that surrounded Christmas. Hugh went to work, but the file was small and the task so great that several nights of work produced only small creases in the heavy iron. He knew that he must be ready when the scheduled day arrived so he kept working steadily, grinding away at the metal during the sleepless dark hours and secreting the file beneath his bunk throughout the day. Christmas and New Year's passed with Hugh making better progress. Two days before the Epiphany he had all but completed the job, leaving the last shreds of metal for severance at the final moment.

Then Captain Leeds paid him a sudden visit!

When he walked into the cell, Hugh trembled with anxiety. The captain sat down on the cot directly over the hidden file and grinned in his repugnant way.

Hugh wondered if he had discovered the plot and was toying with him before the cruel revelation. Perhaps the English jailor had confessed and divulged the entire scheme.

At last Hugh blurted out, "Well, sir, what a pleasant surprise. What errand brings you now to my humble abode?"

Leeds surprised him with an almost-gentle smile. "Tut, tut," he said, "that's no way to greet a man who brings you news. And yet I'm afraid the news will make you unhappy." He pursed his lips in mock dejection and idly fingered the thin bed covering. Did he suspect?

"Get on your feet when you're spoken to!" Leeds commanded sharply.

Hugh had absently seated himself on his stool and now rose. The chains rattled on the flagstones and the rough edges of the weakened bracelets cut his legs beneath his long trousers. Leeds looked him up and down and grinned.

"I doubt if you could be of much use to your parents anyway," he said, with a show of disinterest.

Hugh's cheeks flushed and he spoke quickly. "What about my parents?"

"Ah, they are well enough now, but that condition may be short-lived. In the morning a small fleet leaves Dublin for Donegal Castle. An English regiment will be aboard and I have the privilege of commanding one of the companies. Such a nice time of year for a cruise, don't you think? But do not fret. We shall not be long. I doubt that your fortress can hold out against us."

Hugh was overcome with anger but controlled the temptation to attack his tormentor.

Leeds continued. "A pity, a real pity. But perhaps now we shall have a few companions for you. You may thank your mother's industry in your behalf for this sudden turn of events. She has armed the province and is daily adding new troops from among the peasants. We shall strike before her organization is complete. I think I shall enjoy meeting the rest of your family almost as much as I have enjoyed our own charming relationship." He laughed, got up, and gave the room another look. "Do sleep well," he said and stepped from the chamber.

Hugh sank to the cot and buried his face in his hands. Then he jumped up and paced back and forth in the cell within the limits permitted by the chains, clenching and unclenching his fists as he walked. "They are swine," he muttered, "and Leeds is the worst of the lot. But he is the one that has the surprise coming. This escape must succeed." He banged one hand into another to drive the point home to himself.

He lay awake that night while visions of a burning Donegal filled his mind. He repeated over and over, "I must make it this time! I must!" His impatience mounted with each hour. Outside a light snow began to fall, some of the flakes drifting into his cold cell. Each flake seemed to be a second in eternity and Hugh tolled them off from his couch in order to hasten the loitering hours. The dim embers of his fireplace turned ashen but he did not stir to rekindle them. Throughout the still, white evening he lay restless on the cot, his thoughts churning through the snow to a besieged castle under the command of a brave woman and her sickly spouse. He could almost hear the voice of the Dark Lady riding each gust of wind and calling him back to the North. It was not until dawn that he managed to fall asleep.

chapter 11

THE SNOW CONTINUED to fall throughout
the next day, and the eve of the Epiphany—Janu-
ary 6, 1592—saw Dublin the center of a savage blizzard. Again the weather proved favorable for an
escape from the castle but promised to add to the
difficulties expected on the journey south. A thin
cloud of snow sifted into Red Hugh's chamber as he
applied the worn file to his shackles for the last
time. After a few anxious strokes the bracelets fell
from his legs and he rubbed the swollen ankles to
renew the circulation.

For a while he merely walked up and down in the
room in enjoyment of these first pleasant moments
of relative freedom. Then he dragged his stool to the
window and carefully surveyed the prison yard and
castle walls. He noted that the towers were all manned
by sentinels protected from the weather by their heavy
fur capes. Archers watched the entire expanse of the
square and a squad of pikemen squatted about a fire
near the main gate. Escape would not go undetected
this time if the same plan were followed. Perhaps

Henry and Art had another scheme. Hugh was now eager to embark on most any venture.

As he watched, he spied Captain Leeds riding out of the castle before a large body of cavalry. More troops would join them at the shore and then the entire force would sail for Donegal. If only his people could hold out until he returned to them. He could hear the tower guards celebrating the feast day in song and laughter. Their voices drifted up from the room below. Here was another barrier to their escape.

This reverie was interrupted by a low knock on the door. Hugh hurriedly returned to his cot and placed the fractured bits of steel about his legs. The heavy portal swung open to reveal Henry O'Neill and his brother, followed closely by the English hireling. His friends beckoned him to follow and then retreated slowly down the long hall. Hugh closed his cell door quietly behind him and followed them.

The Englishman had a lengthy coil of rope about his shoulders and the two brothers were equipped with swords and pistols. Art handed Hugh an extra sword and his heart leapt to feel the bright blade in his hand once more. The four men crept cautiously down the stairs past the riotous guardroom without discovery. They found themselves on the dimly lit ground floor of the tower. Art O'Neill moved toward the doorway to view the prison interior.

Hugh warned him, "The place is alive with sentries. We'll never make it that way."

Henry nodded. "We expected that," he said. "That's

why we chose an alternate route." He motioned for them to follow him to a far corner of the compartment and there he pointed to a circular steel disk set in the floor.

"This leads to the sewer that feeds the moat," he explained. "It's nearly dry now and shouldn't hinder us much. We'll descend by the rope—Art first, then you, Hugh, our English friend here, and myself. Let's be off and good luck."

Henry and Hugh dragged the heavy lid from the hole and, after fastening one end of the rope to the bars of a nearby window, they dropped it down into the darkness. Art began to descend laboriously, placing one hand slowly beneath the other. His breathing was harsh and at intervals he had to stifle a cough. He was still not well but he realized the urgency of the escape and sought to do his part as well as possible. As soon as he had reached the sewer in safety he tugged at the rope and Hugh swung out into space. The guard followed him into the pit and then Henry, who left the rope as it was, hoping that it would not be noticed immediately in that gloomy corner of the chamber.

The sewer was damp and narrow and the stagnant water oozed around their knees as they edged along toward the moat. Art's dry coughing echoed in the hollow tunnel and caused the nervous warder to grumble at every sound. They reached the ditch outside the prison wall and crept along the enclosure until they were directly beneath the Birmingham Tower. For a full ten minutes they kept their eyes fixed on the tower sentry. He seemed to be staring right at them but finally he moved to the other side of the parapet to scan the courtyard.

"Now!" rasped Henry, and the four sprinted for the cover of the neighboring street. Here they were to meet Martin with the horses.

With the snow whirling about them they reached the appointed place. The shanachie was here, but he was alone.

"I had the horses with me," he explained sadly, "but I was stopped early this morning by two English officers who questioned me about them. They were heading north, Master Hugh, to attack Donegal Castle."

Hugh nodded.

"Well," Martin continued, "I had to tell them I was bringing the horses to be sold in the Dublin market. They offered to buy them and I refused. But they insisted and said they would take them from me if I did not sell. I dared not arouse their suspicions further so—I sold them."

Hugh sensed the disheartening effect this might have on his companions so he adopted a carefree attitude. "It makes no difference. The air is lovely and everything points toward a pleasant hike in the Wicklow Mountains. I have been there and can speak of what I know. Will you join me?" He bowed low and smiled.

The guard thought little of the humor but the

others caught Hugh's spirit and started off down the
snow-swept street. The men were well armed and determined not to surrender without a battle if accosted.
The town's many public buildings and cathedrals, its
mist-dimmed waterways, its narrow flagstone bridges
—all were as one to them. Their goal was outside of
Dublin, not in its colorful interior. To this end they
pressed along the wet, cobbled streets. The few so-
journers who saw them pass could hardly guess that
these were desperate men fleeing from the queen's
prison, for they smiled and joked and gave every appearance of a group of schoolboys on an outing, with
the English guard acting in the capacity of the disturbed teacher. This latter actor viewed each stranger
with apprehension and wished with all his heart that
he had never entered into the bargain. In spite of
their outward joviality, they maintained a rapid pace,
spurred by the seriousness of their mission. The lack
of horses made their position doubly perilous and the
increasing flurries impeded their progress. Yet they
reached the outskirts of Dublin without raising a general alarm.

Here, again, they ran into a thick stone wall with
its gate now firmly bolted in place. The shanachie
had saved some items from his pack, however, and
among them was a short strand of rope, sufficient
to reach the top of the wall and lower them to
earth on the other side. Martin fastened his heavy
sword to one end of the rope and, after several

attempts, managed to lodge the weapon between two ridges in the notched enclosure. With the line thus secured, he began to scale the barrier.

As chance would have it, three members of the town's garrison picked this very moment to stroll by this spot on their evening rounds. The two groups sighted each other at the same instant. The soldiers were uncertain what escapade they had interrupted —perhaps a student prank or a fellow soldier slipping outside the compound to visit a sweetheart. The cold steel that confronted them convinced them that this was not a playful episode and the two factions closed, their blades whipping lightly through the falling snow. The terror-stricken hireling turned to flee and was instantly thrust through. Pitching forward on the fresh snow, he spilled his life's blood within the walls of Dublin and far from the promise of riches.

Now the sides were even for Martin remained on the crest of the wall to watch the outcome of the struggle. He held himself in readiness to aid the Irish boys should they seem to be getting the worst of it.

Hugh had been out of practice with the sword for many a month but he was still master of his weapon. He maneuvered his opponent against the wall by a series of thrusts and counterthrusts. The English soldier tried desperately to fight clear of this position but the prince parried every stroke of his sword. Finally Hugh swept the Englishman's blade into a high arc and darted underneath. The startled foe died without a murmur.

Henry, too, was an expert swordsman and experienced little difficulty in disposing of his adversary. His tactics were different and employed more strength than skill but the same effect was achieved. In a few moments his gleaming saber slashed across the defense of the second soldier and the Englishman fell as silently as the snow itself.

The third member of the English trio was giving Art O'Neill a frantic battle. Art had not his brother's prowess with the sword and the illness had taken a great deal of the vigor from his broad frame. He was cut severely about the arms and blood dripped from a wound in his thigh. But promise of freedom lent an extra strength to his blade and soon he, too, transfixed his opponent and watched in fatal fascination as he slipped to the ground. Somewhat weakened by the loss of blood, Art had to be hauled up to the top of the wall and then lowered to the open field below. Hugh and Henry followed and took a precious moment to bind up Art's wounds before setting forth once more.

Henry looked back at the city and smiled. "Well, that little encounter relieved us of one debt, at least. We'll enter the mountains all Irishmen and without the services of our grasping friend. Still—he did provide the means for our escape and I say we should be grateful."

"Philosophy comes later," Hugh told him and took

him by the arm. "If the whole town isn't after us in a few hours or less, then the English are more stupid than even I give them credit for. Come on!"

The storm persisted in all of its fury and drove icy fragments against the group plodding resolutely southward. Their wet clothes were little protection and only added to their discomfort. Drifts piled high on the roads and covered the floor of the surrounding forests. Along the ridge of the adjacent ranges the overcast changed the shape of the peaks with each successive gust of wind. The temperature fell and the wind-driven snow nearly blinded them. Their decision had been to keep to the woods and hills, where the footing was more treacherous and the direction more difficult to maintain.

Hugh recalled some familiar landmarks from his first journey—the Dodder, the rock-strewn pass of Glencree, the Two Rock Mountain, and the winding stream of Glencree. Snow blurred the outline of every feature of the land. They passed over bogs glimmering white, through ravines, among the sculptured drifts on the slopes. Martin, hardy and tireless, kept the lead. Together they entered the woods that anchored the foot of the valley. Half blinded by the snow they groped their way among the weighted pines, stumbling often but continually pressing on.

When they paused briefly by a large oak to rest themselves, Hugh made a discovery. "Where's Henry?" he asked, noticing that the younger O'Neill was missing.

Art and Martin had not missed their companion until now and could not tell when he had disappeared. Now all three retraced their steps through the woods, losing valuable time in the process, but they could see no sign of Henry. The fresh snow erased any marks that might have diverged from their own slender trail. To retreat much farther might mean recapture and there was danger in calling aloud in the white forest.

"He will be all right," said Martin. "And better fed than we shall be. He was carrying our food supplies with him. No doubt we'll meet in Glenmalure."

Finally and reluctantly they gave up the search and continued on their way, keeping close together in order to avoid further mishap. Their path led through many a wooded glade and along the courses of several Wicklow rivers which crossed and recrossed, emptying into one another or driving on toward the sea beneath a surface of glass. Now and then an ice-locked waterfall added a touch of fairyland. A few frightened deer peered out from their pale refuge and then bounded off. Other smaller game and weather-worn birds fled before them.

For a while they debated turning off to the domain of O'Toole for sanctuary. Hugh remembered the chief's promise for help at a future time. Now, however, they decided against it for fear that escape in that direction would be cut off and for fear that O'Toole himself, long an antagonist of the English, might now be in their hands as part of a trap. The

Dubliners would expect them to head there. So they trudged on to more distant country.

Slowly Art O'Neill began to fall behind. His wounds and sickness began to affect him and his breathing came with great effort. Red Hugh dropped back by his side and tried to cheer him.

"We've come a long way, Art, and we have but a little farther to the security of Irish arms. Good St. Brendan is with us."

Art nodded feebly and tried to struggle on. He dragged along, his arm on Hugh Roe's shoulder, the prince slowing his step to accommodate him. In that fashion they limped past War Hill and Douce Mountain and plunged into the snow-fed swamp at the foot of these slopes. Martin, too, dropped back to assist Art, who hobbled along between his two friends, his head swinging freely from side to side and his dry lips muttering snatches of songs and prayers.

Martin gave Hugh a worried glance. "He won't last much longer in this," he warned.

"We'll go on as long as we can," said Hugh, but his brow, too, wore a troubled frown.

They had plodded on for a night and a day, and night was again falling. A slow, laborious pace was all they could manage for Art's weight had taxed Hugh's remaining strength and now most of the burden was left to Martin. They had left the wooded shores of Lough Tay with its steep, enclosing mountain walls and crept miserably by the long sheet of ridge-locked water known as Lough Dan, where the scenery was rich and wild. The blizzard now increased in fury. The fugitives had no food so they scooped snow with their hands and made it do for food and drink. Hunger now added to the miseries plaguing Art O'Neill and drove him to his knees where he sobbed convulsively. Hugh was too weak to help him to his feet and stood there tottering in the fierce gale.

"It's no use," he gasped. "We can go no further." His voice was a whisper in the storm but Martin saw submission in his eyes and knew that he spoke the truth.

They had stopped high on Table Mountain, making a strange picture in that savage setting—two tired, suffering, hungry young men in the throes of defeat and a third standing by, powerless to help them. Hugh slumped into the white drift beside Art and called faintly to Martin.

"You'll have to go it alone to Glenmalure. There you will find the chieftain O'Byrne. Have him return for us with horses."

The shanachie protested very little. At Hugh's suggestion he dragged Art across the crusted snow to a shallow cave which dipped for a few feet into the side of the cliff. Hugh hauled his weary body to the same spot and lay down.

"Leave us, now," he said, "and may God and St. Patrick speed you on your journey."

"It shall be but a time until I return," Martin promised. "God keep you for Donegal, my master."

The young prince watched their last hope of survival half-walking, half-sliding down the side of the hill and he kept him in sight until snow flurries obscured the view. Flake by flake, the snow advanced upon the reclining figures and brought the chilling pain of dreamless sleep. The white crystals dived noiselessly into Lough Dan and lost their identity upon the floor of ice. The wind, whining past the rude shelter, made the only sound.

chapter 12

IN THE MORNING a cold mist rose from the ice-bound lake and gave an unearthly appearance to the countryside. No sun shone and, though the storm had ceased, the threat of renewed flurries hung in the leaden sky.

Hugh awoke first and struggled to sit up. His body trembled with the cold and even his head shook like wheat before the wind. Screening his eyes against the snow, he looked down at his companion. Art was lying face down on the floor of the cave. Hugh, startled, turned him over on his back and felt for his pulse. The beat was slow.

"Art, Art," he called as loudly as he dared. "Wake up. Art. It's me, Hugh!"

The frail form stirred and, with an effort, managed a weak smile. His eyes were partly closed and he began to speak in a tone that was barely audible.

"I'm cold, Hugh. Light the fire," he said. "And where's Henry? Father will be angry. He'll get no supper. Light the fire. And the food—and the fire." His voice trailed off. The smile faded and he drifted back into unconsciousness.

Hugh shook his head. "Poor lad," he said to himself. "But cheer up. We'll make it yet."

Then, like a sword thrust, it struck him that neither of them had eaten for more than a day. He decided that he must try to locate some food to keep them alive until O'Byrne arrived with the horses. But when he tried to get to his feet he found that his legs would not support him. One foot felt like it was on fire and the other was beyond pain and feeling. He sank down again and leaned back against the wall of the shelter. With his cupped hands he scooped up a little snow to force between the cracked lips of his friend and then he, too, made a doubtful breakfast of it.

The liquid did a bit to revive him and cleared his mind so that he could think. He realized that their position here was dangerous and becoming worse. Not only the English soldiers but nature itself was tracking them down with a look of malice in her eye. They would freeze to death if not found soon—if they did not starve to death first.

Hugh determined that they should be alive when help came and he made another effort to stand. This, too, failed and he resolved that, if he could not walk, he could at least crawl. Before leaving the shelter, he checked to see that Art was all right and then edged himself over the lip of the cave and began to slide down the side of the mountain using his hands as oars and feet as brakes. It seemed like an eternity before he reached the bottom of the hill and found himself in a dense wood which guarded one of the smaller lakes in the area.

First he discarded his pistol, for the powder had been soaked by the storm and could do him little good. Besides, he would not dare fire the weapon even if the powder were as dry as summer weeds. His short sword would serve to defend them if there was need.

He crept into the woods on his hands and knees and took a position against the base of a giant fir tree. His sword lay in his right hand, ready for action, and his eyes sought out any movement that might herald the approach of small game. For more than two hours he stayed here without seeing a single living thing. Then a rabbit stepped into the white glade.

Hugh made an effort to control himself and waited for the rabbit to come within range. The little creature hopped closer and closer. Then it stopped and looked directly at Hugh, wrinkling its nose suspiciously. Its fears were aroused, but as it turned to leave, Hugh lunged at it with the sword. The rabbit bounded away and Hugh raised himself from the snow more hungry than ever.

He then considered the idea of trapping something and set about hacking down a small tree that stood nearby. From its branches he devised a simple trap, using a strip from his tunic as the trigger mechanism. This took him well into the afternoon and then he sat back and waited.

Nothing stirred in the forest except the speechless

pines which nodded lazily in the freshening breeze. Soon night would be upon them again. Hugh had failed in providing for himself and his companion. He struck angrily at the trap with his sword and buried the blade deep in the snow. When he retrieved it he noticed grass sticking to it.

Grass! It might not be fit for the tables of kings but it could serve to keep them alive. He dug beneath the icy crust and pulled up huge handfuls which he tucked inside his tunic. Then he made his way slowly out of the woods.

For every step Hugh took forward he seemed to slide back half a step. Each movement of his body brought a new sensation of pain. He was now dependent on his arms for all the work. His legs would not respond to the demands he placed upon them. Somehow he managed to propel himself up the slope.

Night was already in command of the landscape when he reached the small cave and there his blood froze in his veins. Art O'Neill was gone! In the dim light he could make out the path that he had taken. It wound around the mountain to the east and Hugh began to crawl wearily in that direction.

He had gone perhaps a quarter of a mile when he spotted his companion lying grotesquely on the surface of the snow. With renewed effort, he hurried to him and lifted him to a sitting position. Art stared straight ahead and took his breath in rapid, uneven gasps. Suddenly he screamed and made an attempt to rise.

"Henry! They've killed him! They've killed my brother!" he shouted and waved his arms wildly.

"He's mad," Hugh thought, "mad as a Killarney lark."

Art's anger quickly subsided and he slowly turned to Hugh and studied him. Then he leaned on Hugh's shoulder and wept. "Henry!" he sobbed. "You've come back for me. Light the fire and bring me some food. I will ask father to forgive you."

Hugh patted his friend affectionately and quietly helped him back to the mountain hollow. Here he attempted to get Art to eat the grass he had brought with him.

"Eat something, no matter what," he reasoned with him. "The brute animals feed on leaves and grass, Art. And while we can think, we are also animals."

Art nodded and smiled but he would not eat. Hugh tried some of the unfamiliar food himself and then lay down to sleep after the long ordeal. He was awakened by Art calling softly, "Henry!"

Humoring his friend, Hugh answered, "Yes, my brother."

"I shall eat now, Henry. You may bring me something to eat."

Hugh smiled sleepily and produced a little of the grass from his day's work. Art nibbled on it greedily for a few minutes and asked, "What is this, Henry?"

"It is—" Hugh faltered. "It's a northern delicacy sent to us by Hugh, the prince of Donegal."

Art nodded in approval. "Oh, I must thank him when next I see him. We were once in prison together. But we escaped and—and—and we were lost in a storm—and—" Again he looked frantically about him and began to whimper like a child.

Hugh cradled Art in his arms and kept him there until they both fell asleep.

With the new dawn, Art was much worse. Hugh could not get him to eat the bit of grass that remained and was barely able to force some snow between his lips. Art was not raving now. His eyes looked straight ahead as if fixed on some sad and frightening spectacle.

Hugh did not venture as far from the cave this day. He searched for hours for some kind of nourishment on the sides of the hill and found only some leaves and a bit of wild mountain grass. These he took with him back to the cave and offered them to Art, but he refused to eat.

The snow had begun to fall again. This time the flurries were heavy but the wind was not so strong. Still they added to the discomfort and blotted out a view of the valley. The cave was little shelter against the elements and Hugh's thoughts traveled back to his own warm home and the cozy room from which he often looked out upon the calm Bay of Donegal. Then the snow was pleasant to watch as it dropped from the heavens with its promise of winter sport and happy hours. Pleasant, too, had been the winters near Lough Swilly where he and Kathleen had skimmed across the ice on wooden skates and coasted, on the shields of her father, down the gentle hills, splitting the mountains with their laughter. Now the snow was an enemy to be feared and hated.

Yet he was better off than Art. How long would it be before he too became as helpless? Desperately, he dragged up some of the leaves from the floor of the cave and began to chew them slowly. It was then that he saw them!

At the foot of the mountain was a company of English dragoons. They were having difficulty in the open country and moved very slowly but their eyes were everywhere.

Hugh dragged Art back against the rear wall of the shelter and prayed that he would not call out and reveal their hiding place. He stretched himself out on the floor of the cave and watched the activity below. The cavalrymen were searching every bit of ground for some sign of the prisoners. No tracks remained, as far as Hugh could tell, but perhaps there would be other signs.

Soon one of the horsemen came bounding out of the glade with Hugh's discarded pistol and presented it to the unit commander. The officer evidently recognized it and ordered a thorough search of the area. In this search Hugh's makeshift trap was discovered and the English pieced together the story of his hunting expedition.

Some of the cavalrymen were sent into the woods, others to search the shores of the lake, and still others to scour the mountain region. Hugh ducked back inside the shelter and, with some difficulty, managed to get Art to lie down. Working as rapidly as possible he covered both of them with a thin layer of snow and lay quite still. One hand steadied Art and the other rested upon his sword hilt. He was determined that they should not be returned to the Birmingham Tower. He told himself that his escape this time would end differently—either in death or deliverance.

The mounted men found the going rugged on the slippery mountainside and did not conduct as thorough a search as they should have. Even so, twice a horseman passed so close to the hidden cave that Hugh might have reached out and caught his stirrup. The searchers finally retreated down the mountain and reported their failure to their leader. The reconnoitering had taken several hours but had proved fruitless. Still the commander was not satisfied. He ordered the men to dismount and pitch their camp in the woods. The search would be continued in the morning.

Hugh's heart sank within him. Now, besides the hunger and cold that had been plaguing them, a more formidable enemy was near. He must think. And he must hope. There would be a way out of this if he could only think. But the lack of food and the chill that was setting into his entire system began to take effect. His head swam and the white flakes danced before his eyes. First his mind became dull and limp and then his body. Crumbling down beside Art, he found himself powerless to rise. He was aware that the snow was drifting in and covering them, yet the only movement he could manage was to wrap his arms about Art. Together now, they fell into the sleep that precedes death, and soon nothing was left between them and the cold. Their bedclothes and their pillows were high, white-bordered mounds of frozen hail congealing all around them. Their light tunics and threadbare shirts were frozen to their bodies and their shoes and fastenings to their legs and feet. They seemed to become only life-size sods of earth covered up by the snow.

Below, the English soldiers sang around their campfires, ate freely of their rations, and then crept beneath blankets placed carefully near the warm embers. They, too, fell asleep.

chapteR 13

WHILE THE ENGLISH slept, a small band of Irish horsemen made their way around the eastern edge of Lough Dan and moved silently up the slope. Leading them was the faithful Martin of Cloghan and at either side rode the chieftains O'Toole and O'Byrne. O'Toole had been in the mountains searching for Hugh when Feach O'Byrne and his men joined him. Surely God was with the shanachie, for he came across the little band just this side of Glenmalure and, with scarcely a word of explanation, persuaded them to follow him to Table Mountain.

They plodded noiselessly past the slumbering sentries and carefully approached the shelter.

Art and Hugh were so deeply wrapped in snow that the rescue party nearly passed them by. Both boys were as still as the night itself and Martin feared that they had come too late.

"Lift them up!" O'Toole commanded softly. "Rub their limbs and try to bring life to them."

As the soldiers did as they were bidden Art O'Neill sat suddenly erect, smiled and then tumbled back into the arms of his rescuers. He was beyond all assistance. The imprisonment, battle wounds, and perilous journey had at last taken their toll and he gasped out his life that white evening in the company of his friends and countrymen.

Working rapidly, O'Toole himself sought to bring Hugh back to consciousness. Feach O'Byrne assisted him, pressing his gloved hands against Hugh's temples. It was no easy task but they were finally rewarded by the slow twitching of his whole body and the slight fluttering of his eyes. The faces of the rescue party circled lazily before Hugh like figures on a spinning shield and their voices came to him like drowsy echoes.

They wrapped him in a broad fur cape and pressed a cup of brandy to his lips. And as he revived, Hugh thanked his friends weakly and then asked about Art O'Neill. Their glances led his eyes to the inert form that sprawled on the snow a short distance away.

"Dead?"

O'Toole nodded. He thrust his fat hands in his belt and turned away as Hugh fought back the tears.

"Come, boy!" O'Byrne said gently. "We must be well on our way by dawn and it will be a difficult ride for you."

Hugh shook his head sadly and would not leave Art's side. His own arms and legs were useless and the loss of Art seemed to drain the last bit of strength from him.

But the grizzled Wicklow chief ordered him lifted

to a horse and directed several of his men in whispers to prepare a grave for Art. Both jobs were accomplished quickly. Hugh was draped across the saddle of one of the two extra mounts and lashed to the horse to prevent a fall. Martin took the bridle and led him away from the gravediggers.

The mountain earth was hard and O'Byrne's men had to content themselves with scraping the snow and topsoil from the ground for a shallow grave. They said a few hurried prayers for the soul of Art O'Neill and the chieftain promised that a more suitable burial would be conducted when the present danger was past. O'Byrne gave the word for his men to mount and signalled the column forward. The lonely mountain wind did the only chanting over the white tomb.

A grim procession now moved down the mountain slope, past the unsuspecting English, by the glassy Lough Dan, and through Glendalough where the stout stone churches gave testimony that the followers of St. Kevin were still hard at work. Here O'Toole left them and a monk who possessed some medical skill was added to the party.

Heading south, they crept past slumbering cottages and beneath the rugged cliffs which bordered the town of the two lakes, on up the white road between the high hedges, and beyond the snug dwellings. Several donkey-cart drivers saluted them and a herd of ill-fed cattle separated to let them through. A fine snow accompanied them and served as a screen to their action. Soon they sighted Glenmalure, a place of wild beauty, flanked by giant peaks which on the western side ended in the great mass of Lugnaquilla, the monarch of the Wicklow Mountains. The Avonbeg, or "little river," spouted from Table Mountain at the head of the valley and continued its course through the town to join the Avenmore at the "Meeting of the Waters" near Avoca. Here, at the eastern edge of Glenmalure, was the stronghold of O'Byrne, high on the side of Ballinacor Mountain.

Moments after their arrival at the castle, O'Byrne dispatched a messenger to the North to tell Hugh's parents that he was safe in Glenmalure. They posted guards at the far reaches of the territory and then they set about the task of making Hugh well again. He was carried to the chamber set aside for the chieftain himself and there the skilled monk attended him. His shanachie, too, remained with him to comfort him. Hugh was still in shock from exposure and from the experiences of the past few days. They laid him on the massive canopied bed and tried to determine his condition.

After a time the monk turned to O'Byrne and said, "He's a lucky lad, right enough. He'll pull through. His limbs are sound except for the right foot where I fear some infection has set in."

"Can it be stopped?" Martin asked.

"God willing, yes, but we'll have to operate and remove the diseased part."

Hugh heard their conversation as in a dream and

pondered it seriously. It was a rule of the ancient clans that no man with a physical blemish should ever sit on the throne of a kingdom. Leary had lost his rule in Connaught when a tribesman lopped off his ear in combat and O'Reilly of Cavan saw his dreams fade when a fall from his favorite stallion twisted his back. Perhaps a physician in Donegal would be able to save the toes. But this would take time and he could not travel until the pain somehow abated. He felt Martin staring at him as if he read his thoughts. He turned the alternatives over in his mind. Would he risk the loss of the kingship in order to save a kingdom? Put that way, the choice was easier to make.

Finally, Hugh called quietly to the priest. "Do what you must, good Father. There's a meeting in Donegal I'd not like to be missing."

"Musha, my boy," the monk said, "you're after being next to the dead and it's a fortunate one you are to be talking at all. You'll not be well for a time yet and you must have patience. You will not be able to rise tomorrow, or the next day, or the day after. Perhaps not for a long time."

Hugh's courage had already returned. "Aye, Father," he said, "it's patience I was learning those long years in Dublin but I was learning other lessons, too. I'll be in the saddle before this present snow has melted."

The monk looked at O'Byrne and Martin of Cloghan. There would be little support for his rec-

ommendations from these two. He arched his eyebrows, threw up his hands, and sighed. "Let us begin,
then. We do not want to waste any of this young
man's precious time."

The tools of his profession were very few and
scarcely filled the brown cloth purse he removed
from his cincture. He called for boiling water and
clean linen. Then, with a small knife he began to
probe the infected foot very gingerly. Hugh set his
teeth against the pain.

"Sure, you'll not miss the little fellows hardly at
all," the priest said with a sympathetic attempt at
humor.

"It is God's will," said Hugh, "and an O'Donnell,
even thus disfigured, will be more than a match for
his enemies."

"Good lad," said the surgeon, patting him on the
arm. The operation was brief and as painless as the
old man and his limited skill could make it. Hugh
remained conscious throughout, biting his lip until
the blood ran. Yet he uttered not a single cry of
pain. Martin and O'Byrne marveled at his courage
for their own faces had gone pale. When the dis-
eased toes had been removed, the monk treated the
swollen foot with some medicinal herbs, cauterized
it with hot oil, and then bandaged it in the white
linen. Hugh was feverish and soon fell asleep, so he
did not hear the group tiptoe silently out of the
chamber. Martin returned shortly and spent the troubled night at his bedside.

In the morning the pain was still intense and the monk redressed the foot, binding more of the healing agents against the throbbing wounds. It was more than ten days before the healing had progressed enough to allow Hugh to hobble about on a crude crutch which O'Byrne's smithy had constructed for him. This he discarded in another week and joined in the regular routine of the castle, limping daily to the exercise yard to strengthen his sword arm and brush up on his horsemanship. Martin watched carefully to see that he did not overtax his strength or reopen the wound. The shanachie and all who observed were amazed at Hugh's quick recovery. O'Byrne thought he might permit him to leave for Donegal any day.

While this decision was being made, O'Byrne's messenger returned from the North with the news that the English were encamped in and about the monastery near Donegal Castle but that they had made no attack on the stronghold as yet. "They're all around," he said, "like thievin' buzzards. They've cut off help from the neighborin' tribes and are fixin' to move on the castle soon, or I'm a sinner."

"Did you speak to my mother?" Hugh asked him anxiously.

"No, that I did not. Sure, no one could enter the place. But I managed to get word to a village fisherman. He delivered it by sea, right under the noses of the English fleet, and didn't he almost drown himself on the rocks as it was."

"What did you hear of my father?"

"That he is alive but not well. And that the news of your lordship's release cheered him greatly."

Hugh paused a moment and then turned to his benefactor. "Good chieftain, you have been most generous to me and I appreciate your many kindnesses. But now I must go home. I am well and can ride. And Donegal has need of me."

"It shall be even as you say, Red Hugh O'Donnell," O'Byrne agreed. "I would, by my sword, that I could ride along with you. You shall have anything you need from us and Martin will be at your side. Two men on horseback will not attract much attention. A cavalry troop might."

"Once again I am indebted to you," Hugh replied humbly.

For the next two days Hugh and Martin prepared for the journey. From the messenger they learned that more than 500 soldiers under Sir Richard Bingham and Captain Leeds, his second-in-command, had encircled the area about the castle. By sudden sorties and a studied process of starvation, they were reducing the garrison. Aid was cut off and the small English fleet blocked access to the wide bay.

"This one, this Leeds," the messenger volunteered, "he's the worst of the lot, sir, they do say. Burnin' the cottages he is, and plunderin', and murderin' the folks as is loyal to the O'Donnell."

Hugh said simply, "I know the man," but his eyes were a terrible thing to behold.

Hugh plied more information from the rider on troop locations and positions and began at once to map his strategy. Each wrong, real and imagined, that had been committed against his parents would be repaid in steel.

When all arrangements had been completed, O'Byrne took Hugh and his shanachie aside and gave them some final words of caution. The chieftain had a slight hitch in his speech and his angular countenance pinched itself into a concentrated mask.

"We have not been bothered here," he said, "because the English fear to send troops this far into the mountains. But they know you are here, Hugh O'Donnell, and they will expect you to ride for Donegal. Unless I miss my guess, they will have a cordon of soldiers stretched across the breadth of Ireland, guarding every river ford and mountain pass and hiding in every village and town. You, it's true, will have the advantage of surprise. They do not know where and when you will make your move and they cannot be everywhere and always alert."

"Where do you think they'll be strongest?"

"Och, that is difficult to say, but I would think the River Liffey offers the first and, perhaps, the greatest hazards."

Hugh and Martin nodded in agreement.

O'Byrne continued, "Remember that your movements must be completely secret. One false move and you are done for. Even though you might escape in a local action, you will bring down upon yourself all of the English horses in the area. Elizabeth does not take this young man lightly. But I guess you know that."

Nothing more was said between them. They bade O'Byrne farewell, thanking him profusely, and struck out for the far province. Danger awaited them along every foot of the way and the peril would double once the goal had been attained. Still they left in good spirits, singing and laughing and drinking in the crisp winter air. Over the drifting snow that had spelled death but short weeks ago, the travelers now galloped, their armor clinking as merrily as altar bells. Hugh was headed home!

chapter 14

THE ROUTE HAD been decided but Martin and Hugh were ready to make any changes that safety advocated. Their course took them north from Glenmalure below the summit of Lugnaquilla and then west toward the border of Kildare. Slowly and carefully they made their way through the gradually diminishing hills and across the limestone plain.

"And is it back to Dublin you're bent, my prince?" Martin asked, as they rode along.

"Nay, Martin, but we'll pass so close to the city that I'm thinking they'll never guess to look for us."

"Aye, perhaps, and if they do?"

Hugh shrugged. "We'll face that when it comes frowning down at us."

The background of mountains and woods was disturbed but rarely by a small cluster of farm buildings, an occasional village, or by the many Celtic graveyards which shot their stone crosses above the earth like uplifted relics for the wind to kiss. A round Norman tower stood out, pencil-shaped, against the sky near a stream that gestured weakly on its way to join the Liffey. The roar of Pollaphuca Falls lay stilled in the crystal embrace of winter. Here the travelers turned northeast and proceeded in the general direction of Dublin itself.

"I think we should have a try at the river near Lucan," Hugh suggested. "It is close enough to Dublin to be lightly guarded and yet far enough away to keep us clear of the town garrison."

Martin agreed. "As sensible as salt, for the stream narrows there and we could cross it should the bridge be impassable."

This change in direction brought them back into the hills outlying Dublin and they could smell the salt air blowing in from the sea. Hugh tucked the small map he was carrying into his leather pouch. He knew this area well. So far they had not encountered a single soldier and this caused them some concern. They scrutinized every peasant they met for fear he might be a scout for a larger force. But the entire day passed without incident except for the many slips and starts that accompany winter riding.

"Do you suppose, Martin, that there are no English soldiers south of the Liffey?"

"It's possible, but I rather think we are threading a narrow gap between their sentries on the coastal road, the guards at the mountain passes, and the patrols along the River Liffey. Otherwise, we could not have come this far without a struggle."

"Then perhaps," Hugh suggested, "this is far enough before nightfall."

Martin nodded. "We can make camp here for an

hour or two and then approach Lucan from the south."

Both men slipped from their horses and led them into a grove where they could tether the animals and have a chance to stretch their own legs. As they moved about, every twig and dead leaf, stiff with the frost, crackled under their feet and a flight of tenant birds evicted themselves. The wind dropped but they dared not risk a fire. Instead they spread their saddle blankets on the crusted snow and reclined upon them. Here they spent the remaining daylight hours in storytelling to keep their minds from the present danger.

"When last we rode and camped like this, Red Hugh O'Donnell," the shanachie said, "you listened close as a deer to my stories and you liked them."

"I like them still, good Martin, and it was often I thought on them in Dublin Castle. Sure and a lot has happened since those gay days."

Martin nodded. "Aye, it was then you'd be king no matter what. Are you still of the same mind?"

"I am," Hugh said simply. "If it is my father's wish and the will of the people."

"Och, I've no doubt they'll be after you with the crown soon enough, but do you feel yourself, my son, that you're ready for it? There's some as will ask are you the same young boy as went away those four years ago."

Hugh did not answer this for a while. He watched the pale hills bleed in the sunset and heard the cry of a gull flying before a hawk.

"I've no doubt I had all the faults they accused me of," he said at last, "and God knows I may have them still. But I've seen what the English can do to our people, to our country. I've spent the long hours thinking on it and like the page of a monk's book it came bright and clear to me. There's a duty in king-ship, like you said, good Martin, as well as a joy. And the first ofttimes outweighs the last. But I yet reach for that crown because I see in it a chance to gather my people, to unite them, to link them with other tribes of the North in a sharp circle of steel that will blunt the attack of the enemy and sweep them from our green hills and valleys."

"You'd not make the throne a tool of revenge?"

Hugh shook his head once. "No, there's but one man I think on thus and we'll meet at the end of our journey. No, I see this conflict with the English as a thing which must be done, like the removal of a dis-eased member from the body. While they live among us we sicken and die. Our life is in our strength which must harvest the land with our bright blades before we can plant it again."

Martin of Cloghan smiled slowly. "You've not been idle, master," was all he said.

Then they spoke of Donegal again and Martin told him of his parents' grief and their determination.

"Sure, she's a marvel, is your mother. She's kept the province for you by her own will power. She's run it like she ran the house—neat and trim and no foolishness."

"Have you seen much of MacSweeney?" Hugh asked.

"Aye, and his daughter." The poet's eyes twinkled. "She does be more beautiful than ever or my eyes have slept like a bear. She's waited to be queen a long time and she'll not be put off much longer, I warrant."

Hugh did not look up. "Did she speak of me?"

Martin sighed. "That she did, until I'd heard the catalogue of your many virtues and she'd wrung my poor mind dry with questions about your very self. She'd know, she would, how you spent your days with me and what we talked about. But she'd charm a serpent, I believe, and I believe I told her all I could, and more."

Hugh had no other questions. This was enough to evoke the memory he had stifled so long and could now recall without pain. She would be a lady now and would have grown like him. He saw her slight form outlined against the portal of the great hall and she entered as the Queen O'Donnell. The poet, with the sense for these things, recognized the dream and did not disturb it.

At length the shafts of the sun had pulled down behind the coastal ridges and the little woodland shadows merged into one dark mass. The two remounted and struck out for Lucan.

They moved slowly now, turning the horses into the shadows wherever they could and hugging the low hills that were slanting toward the Liffey valley.

Abruptly Hugh reined in his mount and put a restraining hand on Martin's saddle.

"Listen!" he cautioned. The two inclined their
heads forward. A rapid crunching of snow broke
the wintry silence.

"Horses!" Martin said. "They're behind us and
headed this way!"

Both men dug in their spurs and lit out for a
small grove that lay in their path. Once they had its
protection they spun around to watch the road. In a
matter of minutes a troop of English cavalry galloped by.

"Do you suppose they saw us?" Martin asked.

"I think not. Too dark and the road with a hundred tracks on it. Just a patrol by the looks. We'll fall
in behind them at a good distance and trail them to
Lucan."

They left the woods immediately and set out at a
trot. An hour's ride brought them within sight of the
river town. Campfires fronted the village like a set of
vigil lights. They dismounted and led the horses into
a small covered ravine. Martin offered to go ahead
and see what dangers presented themselves.

But Hugh smiled and said: "No, Martin. I thank
you, but if anyone takes the risk, I'll be that one.
Keep with the horses and it's I'll be back before you
can glimpse one star to fall. If I shouldn't return,
though, by sunrise, then you fly for Glenmalure."

The prince divested himself of his heavy equipment and set out for the town with only a short

knife for protection. About his shoulders he wrapped a worn cloak so that he would appear to be a poor peasant stumbling in from a day's labor. As he walked he made use of a staff cut from a winter-weary tree.

The dozen or more small fires became more distinct now and each little blaze disclosed its own set of occupants—all soldiers of the queen. Hugh stepped up boldly to one group.

"May I warm myself by your fire, sirs?" he asked. "It's a cold night to be about."

One of the soldiers spat at him. "Go on! Find your own fire, you redheaded rascal."

"Easy, Jeremy," said another. "He's only a lad. Come, sit down, boy. There's room."

Hugh said, "Thank you," and moved next to the fire.

"What are you doing out on a night like this?" asked the friendly Englishman.

"Spying, I'll warrant," said the other. "Or stealing."

Hugh ignored him and directed his remarks to his benefactor. "I was riding to Lucan to visit my kinfolk when my horse went lame. I left him in the hills with my belongings. I intend, sure, to get a horse from my uncle in town and fetch my stuff along with me."

"Hadn't you better be off then?" said the unfriendly one. A few of the others laughed.

"Don't mind Jeremy," said the older and kinder soldier. "This little job has stolen the last of the nerves he had. We've been camped here at Lucan for three weeks, freezing the very eyes out of our heads."

"Well now, and it must be an important thing keeps so many fine men here that long a time," Hugh remarked innocently.

The man shrugged. "Important enough, I guess. It's Red Hugh O'Donnell. He's free, you know, and they think he's bound for Donegal."

"Do they now?" asked Hugh. "And wouldn't this be a poor way to go, so close to Dublin and all?"

The old man laughed. "Of course it is!" he said. "That's what bothers us. He's probably a hundred miles to the west right now. But we have our orders and here we stay."

"Do you have to camp out here? Won't they let you use the town?"

"Not a bit of it. It's too risky. Can't tell when you'll wake with a knife in you. Or an ax across your skull. Even some of the young ones, like you, boy, would kill us while we dreamed." He poked Hugh in the chest to emphasize his point.

"That's if we don't get them first," said the one called Jeremy.

"Nonetheless," said the other Englishman, "it's safer here and no one can get into Lucan without passing us. But we won't see Red Hugh O'Donnell. Might as well watch for Patrick again or one of them fairy troops they say do parade at night."

As the firelight flickered on Hugh's face, the Englishmen might have seen a faint smile but, if they did, they took no notice of it. For a time they talked on military subjects, Hugh pretending to have the curiosity of a farm boy while he learned their strength and their weakness. When he had found out all that he could and had warmed himself clean through, he walked quietly away from the group and entered Lucan. The town was still and things were as the old soldier had said. No troops were billeted here. Hugh then doubled back to rejoin Martin, being careful to avoid the sentries with whom he had visited.

When he arrived at the ravine he told his anxious friend the things he had heard.

"Perhaps we had better skirt the city, Hugh, since all the troops are camped on this side."

"On the contrary, Martin. I think we can pass safely through the heart of Lucan."

Martin looked at Hugh strangely for a moment and then said in resignation, "Let's be off then, before I start listening for the banshee howling around my certain grave."

Hugh laughed and the two mounted together and retraced the path Hugh had taken on foot. It led them to the same campfire where Hugh had spent the last two hours.

"Back again?" the friendly Englishman remarked.

"Passing by is all," Hugh said. "This is my uncle, Martin, who lives in Lucan."

"Strange, I didn't see you return this way."

"True it is. For didn't we lose our way, and my

uncle here brought up in this very place? But we
found ourselves again and will be sleeping tonight in
the city."

"Hmm," the soldier mused. "And where might
your horse be that was lame?"

"Musha, now, and that's the pity of it. We had to
leave him in the mountains. Too hard traveling by
night. In the morning we'll fetch him."

The Englishman regarded them carefully as if
turning their fate over in his mind and then waved
them on. Relieved, the fugitives walked their mounts
through the soggy city streets and passed over the
Liffey without ceremony. Five thousand men at arms
kept watch along the stream for just such a crossing
but Hugh Roe and his shanachie met with not so
much as a challenge as they stepped onto the northern bank. Donegal was still a long way off, however,
and but one perilous area had been mastered.

The next important barrier was the Boyne River
which lay some twenty-five miles to the north. They
stayed about ten miles inland, keeping to the unfre-
quented roads and bearing in the direction of
Drogheda which straddled the Boyne. They rode
past squat little farmhouses where the toil of the
winter months had moved indoors. Across the stub-
ble fields and pastures they saw the hay yards, filled
with ricks of hay and grain, nestling against the
farm buildings and the houses beyond. Occasionally
a herdsman, shivering at his task, tucked a greeting

into his nod, unaware that it was the prince of Donegal sweeping gaily past.

A light breeze came up and caused the thin blanket of snow to shift and swirl about the horses. Both travelers began to hunger for a warm fire and some hot food. Deciding to chance the delay, they stopped at one likely looking cottage to ask for the traditional Irish hospitality accorded all wayfarers. The house was weather-worn and ugly, but smoke curling from a stunted chimney gave evidence of a fire within. Under an overturned cart a cluster of hens gathered and blinked at the intruders. Hugh knocked on the wrinkled door.

It opened a crack and a fat little face peered nervously at them.

"Who be you?" asked the old woman regarding them suspiciously.

"Countrymen!" Hugh replied, "and we've traveled far. We'll pay you for what we eat."

"No need for that, lad," the matron said peevishly, "for it's welcome you are to what poor food we have. It's only a body has to be careful these days, what with the English swarming all over this land like maggots looking for that O'Donnell boy."

"What? Haven't they caught him yet?" Hugh asked, with a wink to his companion.

"Och! No fear of that," the woman said, ushering them into her humble dwelling. "That boy is blessed. Sure, didn't he fly right out of Dublin Castle with them English soldiers watching all about? Now it wouldn't surprise me none if he's changed hisself into a bird and is on the wing to Donegal right now."

"Even a bird gets hungry," Hugh said softly to Martin.

"Eh?" the hostess asked.

"I said it's a burden to be so hungry."

Martin coughed back a chuckle.

The travelers sat down at a plain table where two wooden bowls and a pair of ashen cups were laid before them. A bed of rushes covered with skins occupied one corner and a weak peat fire flickered at the far end of the dim room. Some well-worn farm implements hung on the turf walls and a sleepy puppy opened one eye to inspect them. A stillness fell over the poor but tidy home as the Irish mistress disappeared into the kitchen to prepare some food.

Abruptly Martin glanced up and signaled Hugh with his eyes. The prince turned slowly toward the curtained door which separated the kitchen from their quarters and noticed a pair of boots protruding beneath the heavy drape. The feet were withdrawn hurriedly and the fugitives faced one another again, saying nothing. From the corner of his eye Hugh caught a glimpse of a figure moving across the yard from the house to the barn. The stranger stopped by the horses and, with a hasty glance toward the house, began to examine them.

"What have we walked into?" Hugh wondered. Perhaps this was a trap that had been prepared in many homes along the route. Or perhaps the owner of the cottage was on his way to inform on them to the English.

The return of their hostess stopped all speculation.

"You live here alone?" Hugh asked.

The woman paused and then answered slowly, "No. Husband's in the barn. He'll be along after he looks to your horses."

She placed some oat porridge before them and some dry bread. As a delicacy she added a bowl of acorns.

"I apologize for my simple table," she said quietly.

"It's fine," Hugh told her, "and such as we're used to."

"Is that true now? And here I'd taken you for two men such as would live in castles and the like."

Martin shot a glance at Hugh but the prince calmly studied a spoonful of the cereal and then looked straight at the hostess. "So that's what you take us for, good woman, is it?" he demanded.

The housewife became frightened. "Sure, I should think you'd be pleased," she stammered.

"Pleased, is it? Two men such as we are with the toil of the years on our faces being taken for a pair of worthless noblemen. Why, it's farmers we are, like yourselves, and it's many a long year my uncle here and myself have spent on a plot of land very like yours."

"Except for those years you spent in prison, Red

Hugh O'Donnell," said a new voice from behind the curtain.

Hugh and Martin rose quickly and drew their swords. The farmer was pushed gently through the opening in the curtain and his wife ran to him and clung to his arm. Then a hand reached out to draw back the curtain and reveal the owner of the strange, yet familiar, voice.

chapteR 15

THE SILENCE WAS broken by a bright, cheerful laugh. "Now isn't that a fine way to greet an old friend?" MacSweeney asked as he stepped into the room.

Hugh rushed to the North country giant and took his broad hand in both of his. It was the same MacSweeney of the Battle-Axes—his hair now streaked a bit with gray, his arms showing a few scars—but the same powerful figure who still held the same inspirational quality for Hugh.

The men shook hands all around and the frightened hostess smiled for the first time.

"How did you know you should look for us here?" Hugh asked his old tutor.

"A lucky accident," MacSweeney answered. "First, I was informed you passed through Lucan—"

"But how—"

MacSweeney raised his hand to stop the question. "We have friends everywhere, Hugh. But do not worry. The English think you're still south of the Liffey."

"But why, old friend, why were you seeking for me?"

"It's a long story, lad, and not a very happy one. We fought the English once outside Donegal and they scattered my men to the hills. Your people are safe inside the walls of the castle but their food supply is low and I'm thinking it will not be long until the English try to force their way into your fortress. I've gathered my men near Ballyshannon. Not too many of them, but they're ready for a fight. Then I thought I'd best be looking for you just so's you wouldn't miss the fun. Had to be careful till I was sure it was yourself. And that's about the length and breadth of it."

The chieftain joined Hugh and Martin at their meal and the housewife flitted here and there attending to the needs of her special guests. The cakes and brimful cups of milk followed the bread and cereal. Soon they had finished, thanked the old couple for their hospitality, and took their leave. MacSweeney led out his stallion that had been hidden in the stable and rode beside the others.

They quickened their pace in order to reach Drogheda by nightfall. Their path took them closer to the rugged coast line of Meath. Here the strong air and the gulls flooded the mind of the Donegal boy with memories. Soon he would be home again! Home to the Dark Lady, to his father, and to Kathleen. A light snow still hung in the air and freshened it. At length they descended into the Boyne valley and saw the walled town of Drogheda stretched out before them.

"Prince and poet," MacSweeney announced, "this

is where I begin to earn my keep. You'll dismount here, please, and I'll take the horses through town. The place'll be alive with English soldiers but they know me and will suspect nothing. It's alarming what a little drop of gold will do here and there." He smiled wickedly. "You two will go upstream about two miles and you'll find a small boat. Its owner will ferry you across. I'll be waiting for you on the other side."

"Suppose you're caught," Hugh said.

"Then you go on foot to Mellifont, six miles northwest, and ask for Sir Garret Moore. He's English but a friend to the O'Neill. He'll shelter you and provide you with fresh horses. But let's not bury a hound until he's dead. I'll be there to meet you, never fear."

The little group split up and MacSweeney rode through the massive St. Lawrence Gate, the extra mounts tagging along behind him. Hugh and Martin, carrying their saddles and other equipment, made their way along the bank of the Boyne. The path was overgrown with trees and difficult, and it was slippery underfoot. Both men were breathing heavily when they reached the boat. Everything was as MacSweeney had said except the oarsman was sleeping calmly in his currach, snow sifting in all about him, and had to be roused. When Hugh shook him, he sprang to his feet, rubbed his puffy eyes, and cast a worried glance about him.

"Let's be off, my lords," he said. "I'm just a simple

ferryman and don't like to mix in politics. Feel lots safer, I will, when you're on your way again."

"We're anxious to see the other side, too," Martin said, "so cast off when you will."

After the gear was loaded and the travelers settled, the skipper thrust his pole into the bank and shoved his little currach off from the south shore. The Boyne was full of floating ice, making passage both difficult and slow. Twice the unsteady craft nearly capsized. But the ferryman, whatever else he might have been, was a good helmsman and he poled his way safely to the opposite side. When they put ashore, Hugh tried to pay the man from his meager purse but the ferryman declined.

"It's glad I am to do a favor for you and for O'Neill," he said through a yawn. "And as happy to trick the English." Then, as he pulled back for the opposite side, he added, "Besides, I already been paid."

The men laughed and then clambered up the white bank dragging their gear behind them. True to his word, MacSweeney was waiting with the horses. As they saddled up, the chieftain told them he had experienced no difficulty in passing through the town.

"Found out one thing, though," he informed them. "Somehow the English found you crossed at Lucan and they're searching farther north. The sooner we get out of this country, the better."

"Do we ride all night?" Martin asked.

"No, we'll be safe tonight at Mellifont, and a good day's ride tomorrow should see us out of danger."

The six miles to the home of Sir Garret Moore were covered swiftly and the bulky square tower of Mellifont, rising half a hundred feet in the air, guided them in. The snowstorm had become more intense and obscured for Hugh a good view of the Moore home. He saw, however, that the building, originally a monastery, had been cleverly turned into a fortified home and had many of the defenses that characterized a larger keep.

Moore was at the drawbridge to greet them and he led them to the warm hall where the table was set for feasting. The Irishmen were introduced to Lady Moore and to the few loyal soldiers that the lord kept as his personal guard. Then they ate—roast capon and small potatoes browned in butter and wine from the vineyard of Normandy—and, when they had had their fill, they were ushered to spacious chambers where a welcome rest awaited them. Again thoughts of home crowded Hugh's mind. He tried to dismiss the thoughts of the siege and concentrated on the memory of his last night in Donegal and his farewell to his father. How good it would be to see him again! And his mother, Ineen Duive. Then, when he had attended to the affairs of the castle, he would ride on to Lough Swilly.

By cockcrow the three were awake, fed, and on

their way with a fresh set of horses. The storm had worn itself out but it left the roads a foot deep in snow.

"I doubt we'll get to Armagh tonight," MacSweeney said. "It's lucky we'll be to get as far as Dundalk."

"You think they'll have troops that far north?" Martin asked.

"Humph!" MacSweeney replied. "Even saw some north of Armagh when I was on my way to meet you. Course, when they get that far north, they'll run into trouble of their own. Dundalk, though, that's another story. Still plenty of English around Dundalk. We'll have to be careful."

Evidently the English cavalry units were not too anxious to test the snow-covered highways, for the fugitives did not cross the path of a single English troop. Once, passing Ardee, they noted a band of cavalrymen quartered in the town square but this group paid no heed to their flight. The riding was more difficult than it had been on any previous day and even the fresh horses began to tire toward evening. Their riders, too, were ready to refresh their bodies with a little sleep.

"It's here for the night, then?" Hugh asked as they neared Dundalk.

"Aye. As good a place as any. There's an inn here which should be safe enough. We'll be merchants going to Armagh on business."

Dundalk was a busy little town at the head of a wide bay whose waters shaped the coast line into a fist with the index finger pointing west. Many legends of Irish heroes had been woven about its locale.

" 'Twas here, Hugh, that the Red Branch Knights gathered," Martin said. "And they built a great part of the wall that now surrounds the city. Cuchullain won a contest here and Cormac mac Art slew one hundred invaders on these same shores."

The riders were checked briefly at the main gate but their story of business in Armagh was believed, with the assistance of a little MacSweeney gold, and they were allowed to proceed.

The bearded warrior of Swilly led them directly to the inn, a place called "The Shield Bearer," and there one large room was assigned to them. Their horses were taken to the stable by a young Irish groom and the three men, after leaving their heavy clothes and other belongings in their chamber, assembled downstairs to discuss plans for the next day. Broth was served to them by a red-faced, pockmarked innkeeper and, as they sipped the hot liquid, they plotted the remaining miles of their escape.

They had been there no more than thirty minutes when five English soldiers walked in. They had been drinking and were singing loudly as they crossed the hall and tumbled into one of the large lantern-lit booths. Here they continued their song and laughter and called for round after round of drinks. Hugh, Martin, and MacSweeney soon found themselves unable to concentrate and they decided to retire to their room to complete their plans.

They had started for the stairs when one of the drunken soldiers noticed them.

"Hey, look ye there now," he shouted to his companions. "It's a pig with red hair. One of them Irish pigs."

Hugh spun around and confronted the Englishman, but MacSweeney laid a heavy hand on his shoulder. "Be careful, lad," he warned. "Let him alone."

"Good night!" Hugh said evenly to the soldier and turned for the stairs once more.

"No, no!" called the Englishman, lurching from the booth and moving toward Hugh. "I've always wanted to see a pig wait on table. Here! Fill my cup!"

Hugh bit his lip but did not move.

"I said, fill my cup." The soldier belched and struck Hugh across the mouth with the goblet.

Hugh lashed out at his adversary, catching him full on the jaw with his fist and draping him across a low bench. The others struggled to their feet and reached for their weapons. The Irishmen drew their swords.

"We're in for it now, lads," MacSweeney said, smiling grimly. "Make your blows count or this is as far as we go."

The chieftain slashed his way across the room and cornered two of the Englishmen before they could leave the booth. Two men, sober and expert swordsmen, would not have been a match for MacSweeney and these men were neither. One lunged wildly at him and was dispatched with a single counterthrust. The second scrambled to place the table between himself and the warrior. MacSweeney pinned the man's blade to the board, then brought his own sword up quickly, piercing the other's heart.

Martin and Hugh were also experiencing little difficulty. Each had a single adversary and with these they toyed, maneuvering them against the wall and preparing them for the finish. The poet, as talented with the steel as with his tongue, sent his man's sword swinging into the rafters and then thrust his own blade home. Hugh, somewhat hampered by his injured foot in these close quarters, was about to do the same when Martin cried, "Look out, Hugh!"

Hugh turned to see the man he had knocked down rising unsteadily to his feet and lunging at him. He caught the thrust on his own sword hilt and parried it skillfully, throwing his opponent against the wall. Then he turned quickly to face his original enemy. This man, however, on hearing the prince called "Hugh" had dropped his weapon and headed for the door.

"Stop him!" Hugh called. But MacSweeney tripped over the shattered remnants of a table and sprawled headlong. Martin had turned his attention to Hugh's new adversary and had spun him to the floor, disarmed and with a fatal cut across his throat.

The remaining Englishman had slipped the bolt on the door and had dashed into the night crying lustily, "It's Hugh O'Donnell! He's here! Red Hugh is here!"

The frightened innkeeper raised his blotched face above the level of the counter as the three Irishmen ran to their room, reappeared almost immediately, and headed for the stable. A hurried search produced their horses and, mounted once again, they spurred for the north gate of the city. As they raced through the streets of Dundalk many a startled citizen gaped at them and many a candle flashed on in a darkened household. Watchdogs barked and the various sounds of alarm echoed from the far corners of the city.

They reached the gate just as an English lieutenant galloped up to the gate keeper. "Drop the gate and seal off the town," he commanded.

Hugh cut down the officer and MacSweeney dropped the warden with a well-placed kick to his stomach. And they sailed through the opening just as the pointed barrier fell, the spikes plunging into the moist earth with a thud.

"We'll keep to the road, lads," MacSweeney yelled. "They'll be after us anyway and we'd best make what time we can!"

They dug in their spurs and rode as hard as they dared. Behind them the bells sounded sharply and they guessed that pursuit would be a matter of minutes.

"Come on! Now, boy, now," they clucked to their mounts, pleading with them as they churned up the white highway that led to safety. First they sped northwest, crossed the border of Armagh county, and then through the small market town of Crossmalgen. A drunken shopkeeper rubbed his eyes and stared. Frozen trout streams and ancient ring forts disappeared in their wake. A herd of shivering cattle looked at them from an enclosed field and, here and there, an English sentry called upon them to halt but did not take up the chase. An occasional shot dug into the snow behind them as they drove on.

The enemy was on the road, however. Near the sloping hills that led out of Cullyhanna they spotted a large troop of cavalry about two miles behind them and rapidly closing the gap. Push as they might, they could not keep the pursuers from narrowing the distance. On toward Keady they fled, weaving in and out of the diminutive hills that filled the landscape. Antique burial grounds and pre-Christian ruins lay smothered in snow beside the road and muffled the sound of the hunters and the hunted.

The Irishmen yelled at their horses, caressed them, goaded them on.

"They're still coming!" Martin shouted, looking over his shoulder.

"Keep moving, lads! We're close to O'Neill territory now and may find some friends," MacSweeney answered him cheerfully.

Down the main street of Keady they flew with the pursuing force less than half a mile behind them.

As they approached the town square with its brood-
ing Gothic cathedral they were surprised by a group
of English horses just entering the street from the
north. This new body of the enemy quickly sized up
the situation and took out after them.

Hugh and Martin followed the hulking chieftain
down a side road and into the open country which
lay east of town. The air was filled with the furious
cries of the English. The Irishmen skirted the edge of
a frozen chain of lakes, plunged through the deep
drifts, and cut north again into the hills. Into a narrow ravine they darted, single file, with the English in
close pursuit. They swept across the base of a low hill
and into a tiny snow-sprinkled valley. To the far end
of the valley they raced and found a narrow winding
path their only way out. They took it. But the trail
was crusted with ice and the tired animals could not
get their footing. They slipped and strained, and slipped some more.

"Here's as good a place as any to die," Hugh called,
drawing his sword and swinging his horse toward
the enemy. His companions joined him, linking their
hands for a moment of well-wishing and then facing
the advance of their hated foe. The English, seeing
their predicament, slowed down their charge and
spread out across the floor of the valley in a thin
line. Then they began to close in.

A light breeze whistled across the glen and wafted
the drifting flakes into the drawn faces of the men at

bay. The steady crunch of the English troops advancing was the only sound.

Suddenly the air was filled with the screams of a hundred men. For a second Hugh thought the cries signaled the English charge but now the words became more clear. "The Red Hand for Erin!" was the welcome phrase he heard—the war cry of the O'Neill.

Down from the hills they poured, swinging swords and axes. They drove into the slim British line and began to consume it like fire eating at a fuse. Those of the enemy who could flee did so, and spurred out of the glen with the yelping Irish at their heels.

Hugh was safe. Thanks to O'Neill, the Earl of Tyrone, and his men, the escape was at last successful.

chapter 16

HAVING SCATTERED the English forces and
driven them to refuge in Keady, the rescue party
wheeled about and cantered back to their countrymen. MacSweeney was no stranger to them.

One of them called to him. "I thought you'd get
in trouble if you went alone."

Another laughed. "Had we known it was you we
were saving we'd have foregone the pleasure of whipping the English."

Back and forth the banter passed until the warriors had their fill of the jest. Then Hugh and Martin
of Cloghan were introduced and the entire company
set out for O'Neill's camp. The Earl of Tyrone was
in the field rather than in his remarkable fortress at
Dungannon. It seemed that the English in the area
afforded many an opportunity for a skirmish and
this northern chief was not one to pass up a fight.

As they rode through Armagh, Martin pointed
out to Hugh the many wonders of the ancient seat
of kings. Much of the city was in ruins where the
local chieftain, some years before, had destroyed it
rather than let it fall to the English. But even the

ruins were magnificent. The town had a quiet dignity and the well-designed streets, some of them topped with marble, were dominated by twin cathedrals which sat on adjoining hills. It was here in Armagh that the great Queen Macha held sway and here that St. Patrick established his primal church. It was here, also, that Brian Boru was buried near the body of Rori O'Connor, the capital's greatest ruler.

On they pressed through the fertile, well-wooded valley of South Tyrone, across the Blackwater, and on to the camp of the most famous of the Irish chieftains, the O'Neill. The spirited banners of the officers of O'Neill danced in the brisk wind and by each of their tents stood a proud shield. About these tents were gathered a variety of fierce, jovial veterans, their shaggy blankets cast on the ground and their rough voices blended in song or story. The rich aroma of simmering beef filled Hugh's nostrils and his ears rang to all the sounds of an army in the field.

Then, by the green canvas with the broad, brilliant shield of O'Neill nearby, the prince and the king met for the first time. It was a meeting that would change the face of the Irish nation for the next fifty years.

The two men—one young, with flaming hair and a spirit to match, the other older, wiser, and with the restraint of a playful animal about him—clasped hands and squatted before the flap of the tent. O'Neill was a magnificent specimen—a rare combination of mental and physical giant. From beneath his dark eyebrows he surveyed the young Prince of Donegal.

"So you're the lad that's had the English on their heads for weeks!" He accompanied his words with a charming smile.

"Thanks to your men," Hugh said, "I am now rid of that terrible responsibility. We are all indebted to you."

At that moment a familiar figure rushed up to join them. It was Henry O'Neill whom Hugh had seen last on that fateful Epiphany night. The two young men embraced vigorously while the elder O'Neill looked on impatiently.

Immediately Henry asked, "And what of my brother, Art? We were told you came alone. What of him?"

Slowly and sadly Hugh unfolded the story of Art's death, and when he finished, both speaker and audience had tears in their eyes. It was some time before they were able to proceed with their other plans.

Henry gave Hugh an account of his dangerous trek north after losing his companions in the storm. He was plagued by English troops all the way until he crossed the Boyne. There he was met by his father's advance guard and taken home in triumph.

Soon it was time to turn their attention to more serious matters. For several hours the leaders conferred, exchanged information, and drew up plans for a union between the houses of O'Donnell and

O'Neill. Together they fused the steel that proposed to lop off the greedy arm of Elizabeth. Dreams they were now, these plans of conquest, but within the year Ulster would be aflame and the names of O'Neill and O'Donnell would strike terror into the hearts of all loyal to England. Their oath was confirmed on the hilts of their crossed swords, an ancient process making them comrades-in-arms.

Their conference ended, the two warriors parted. Hugh of Donegal joined MacSweeney, Henry O'Neill, and the poet, Martin, by a campfire and spent the darkening hours with them in easy conversation. Before long, however, they wrapped themselves in the fur capes offered by their clansmen and slept beside the coral embers.

No sooner had the first rays of morning lit the world than Hugh was up and ready to write the finish to his journey. Henry asked if he might accompany his friend to Donegal and was given permission to do so by his father. It was a quartet, now that set out first for Enniskillen where Maguire held sway over the province of Fermanagh.

Here the prince was given a brief but royal welcome. Maguire eagerly joined the confederacy initiated by Hugh and the Earl of Tyrone, and he gave Hugh a black polished ship which lay at anchor in Lake Erne. With his party, Hugh embarked on the final leg of his journey, the cruise through Lough Erne to the castle at Ballyshannon. A small fleet accompanied him carrying foot soldiers, or "kern," which the gracious Maguire had lent him for his forthcoming struggle.

The ships plied swiftly through the familiar waters, skirting small islands and myriad peninsulas. Threading their path through miniature ice floes, they passed towering mountains, lakeside villages, curious stone bridges, and river palisades. At length they reached the mouth of the Erne, that pleasant salmon-breeding river, and glided down to the foot of Ballyshannon, another of the O'Donnell castles in the province of Donegal.

As the prince and his followers disembarked they were greeted by the jubilant townspeople. Hugh was swung up into the saddle of a waiting horse and led through the streets where the citizens gathered and sang his praises from the roadside to the rooftops. Their prince was home! Red Hugh O'Donnell had come home!

One of MacSweeney's lieutenants rode up to the group once they had stopped near the Ballyshannon cathedral.

"What news?" MacSweeney asked him.

"None that's pleasant, sure," the officer replied. "We skirmished with some cavalry near Ballintra yesterday forenoon but were driven off. There's a lot of rushing about in their camp. They're up to something, I'm bound."

"Are all the English there at Donegal?" Hugh asked.

"Most of them by the look, sir. Some, though
—maybe one company is all—are quartered in the
monk's place outside the walls a bit."

"The monastery? But where are the good Franciscans?"

"Driven off they were, sir, by this captain and his
men. He's a rough sort, he is."

"A big man, is he? With a raw face and black hair
tumbling about it?"

"The same."

"You know this man, Hugh?" MacSweeney asked.

"I do. It's that Leeds I spoke of. A devil he is and
a debt he yet owes me. Perhaps tomorrow I'll just
make a demand for payment."

"There's hundreds of them there, my boy," the
chieftain said. "It may take a little doing."

"And how many men have you, my old friend,
that we can count on?"

"I'd say five score, no more."

"Ah, and Maguire has lent us about the same
number. That should be more than enough to serve
our cause."

They moved onto the cathedral porch and there
continued their conversation, Hugh astride the rail-
ing where he could wave to the townspeople that
came to gawk at the marvel of his resurrection.

"What we have ahead of us is no seaside picnic,
lad," MacSweeney warned as he spread a crude map
upon the flagstones. "The English are here, here,
and here." He indicated their positions with his

dark finger. "They've guns and plenty of horses and they'll be expecting trouble from one quarter or another."

Hugh studied the sketch carefully, questioned the chieftain at length, and then announced his plan.

"We'll all depart at the first hour of morning. Henry O'Neill will command the fleet and the soldiers of Maguire. Martin, you'll go with him. Bring your ships into Donegal Bay by the Cove of Laghey and wait there for my signal."

Martin asked: "And what signal shall we watch for?"

"In a minute, good Martin," Hugh replied. "I'll head for the monastery with MacSweeney and his men and whatever troops we can gather from among the citizens here."

MacSweeney was for caution. "Wait, boy," he said, "if we attack the small force there, our presence will be discovered and we'll have little chance with our few men when the main body of English strikes back."

"I've thought of that, sire, but I'm counting on not being discovered. We'll lie in wait for the English quartered there and take them prisoner."

MacSweeney shook his head. "A risky business."

"It seems once my foster father taught me that all war was a risk and that victory goes to him who takes the greatest one. Is the pupil now to disobey the master?"

MacSweeney had no answer but a smile.

"Once we have taken the English garrison at the monastery," Hugh went on, "our path to the castle will be clear and we need fear no attack from behind. We shall move on the besieging forces at once. A flaming arrow shall be the signal for the fleet to sail to the castle wharf and take the English on their flank."

"Have not the English a fleet of their own in Donegal Bay?"

"They have, but MacSweeney informs us that it is small, poorly armed, and very much undermanned. The fighting men are ashore."

The northern chieftain nodded in agreement.

"Let us then spend a brief time in studying the details of our plan, some further time in prayer for the success of our venture, and, in what hours are left, sleep against the morrow."

For nearly an hour the officers gathered about the rude chart and compared notes, made suggestions, and outlined responsibilities. Then they dispersed and retired to their separate chambers in the Ballyshannon fortress.

MacSweeney placed a restraining hand on the shoulder of his foster son.

"I'll have you know now, lad," he said, "that I'd some misgivings about your little plan. But now, by the green sod, I believe she'll work. We've a young crew, not long in the fighting harness, but I think we'll account for ourselves."

Hugh took his friend's hand. "It's long I've dreamed

of riding to battle with the MacSweeney on my right. It's the first and not the last blow we'll strike together."

"Here's luck, Red Hugh. And you'll have more than one of my clan wishing you well. I'm afraid my addle-brained daughter gave up the thought of any man but yourself since you both were children by the shores of the lake."

Hugh colored a bit but mastered himself and said, "When I have done here what must be done, I'll ride to Rathmullen and ask her to Donegal as my bride."

MacSweeney laughed. "If you'll curb that impatient tongue of yours, boy, I can save you a trip. Sure, as soon as we landed in Ballyshannon I sent a rider north. I've no doubt the poor girl will be joining us in another day."

Hugh could not hide an embarrassed grin as he studied the twinkle in MacSweeney's eyes. "Thank you," he said quietly and, arm in arm, they strode into the castle.

Throughout the crisp night there were the quiet sounds which veteran soldiers could tell you preceded a battle. Citizens were roused and asked to ride with O'Donnell. Many donned rusty and ill-fitting armor to join the task force then assembling.

Red Hugh knelt by his low cot and prayed for God's blessing on his venture. He asked for light to guide his thinking and strength to sustain his courage. His prayers finished, he climbed into bed and lay for a few moments reflecting on the past four years—his mother and father, his cell in Birmingham Tower, the death of Art O'Neill. Tomorrow he would be home. At the head of an army. A small army, it was true, but an army nonetheless. The dream he had dreamed in his room many years back would now come true. Success or failure—how would it end?

chapter 17

AT ONE HOUR after midnight the soldiers were awakened by a shrill blast of the war trumpet and were soon dressing for combat. Muffled pipes sang a frenzied tune and a lone drum thudded ominously outside the castle wall. Hugh was already up and about, having slept fitfully during the few hours of darkness. In the courtyard a hundred torches threw the shadows of busy warriors against the broad stone walls. The heavy ring of armor, the rasping of the drowsy horses, the quiet commands of the officers filled the square.

Hugh accompanied Henry and Martin to the wharf and watched while they loaded troops and equipment into a dozen small boats.

"You'll remember then," he reminded them, "to assemble at the cove near Laghey and to watch for the fiery arrow."

"Aye," Henry answered. "With the sea as calm as it is and the wind as fair, we look forward to a pleasant sail. Don't do too much work for us, Hugh. We'd like to be in on the finish."

"There'll be plenty for all to do." Hugh smiled and saluted his two friends as they took off.

He followed the ships with his eyes as they rode the swift Erne into the bay and swept north along the coast. Then he hurried back to rejoin MacSweeney and the others. The foot soldiers were already assembled and a moderate unit of cavalry pulled at their mounts to keep them in line.

Dressed in the armor and shield that MacSweeney had brought from Rathmullen, Hugh vaulted into the saddle and signaled the little legion forward. The grizzled chieftain rode beside him in the vanguard and kept a steady eye to either flank where horsemen paced carefully to guard against a surprise attack.

"Three hours to Donegal, would you say?" Hugh asked.

"No more," MacSweeney replied. "We should arrive well before dawn."

"We'll have to surprise the sentries at the monastery and take over the garrison before they can put a foot in their boots."

MacSweeney nodded. "A clever plan, laddie, like I said to you, but it'll take a bit of doin'."

Hugh reprimanded him kindly. "My old friend, you worry like a peasant in a dry season."

The small column moved along the coast in the dim light. To the west of them the surf broke angrily against the rocks and, far above, a dark pattern of honking geese flew beyond the reach of mist or man. Somewhere out there sailed the little flotilla with Henry O'Neill and Martin looking intently across the bow of their flagship. Recent snows had left the coastal roads muddy and the sucking sound of the horses' hooves plodding through the mire was the only sign the Irish were on the march.

The foot soldiers kept to the edges of the road, swinging their long pikes and broad axes in unison. Their faces belonged more to a group of festive hunters than to men of war, and only the silence imposed on their mission seemed to keep them from breaking into song. Their youthful leader rode among them, encouraging them in his quiet manner and keeping their spirits high for the work ahead.

In this way the time passed until the attacking force had skirted east of Laghey and bypassed the lifeless town of Donegal, hypnotized into uneasy slumber by its alien occupants. Through the undulating haze Hugh got his first glimpse in four years of the beloved towers he called home. In one of them, he knew, father and mother slept. If all went well, his arms would be about them in a few hours.

Now the low gray buildings of the monastery loomed up before them and Hugh raised his hand as a signal to halt. He spoke to MacSweeney in a low whisper.

"We'll go ahead and see where the English are quartered. It'll give us a chance to spot the sentries as well. Put someone in charge until we return and tell them to move in if we are not back in a quarter of an hour."

The two men slid forward on foot through the wet fields streaked in white and black.

When they reached the outbuildings of the abbey, the Irishmen dropped on all fours and crept to the nearest little cottage. Peering through a window, they discovered it was deserted. They investigated the other small structures around the perimeter and found them still and empty. Not a sentry had they seen. Not a sound of living creature had they heard, only the wind from the bay gusting softly through the yard, swinging and ringing several of the small bells that stood about the grounds and cracking the frozen branches of the elms. Except for the myriad footprints that clogged the mud- and snow-packed area, there was little evidence of human habitation.

"I don't much like the looks of this," MacSweeney whispered.

"Do you suppose they're in the rectory or the chapel?"

"Hard saying, lad, but there's one way to find out. Come on!"

Keeping well within the shadows, they circled the court and drew up at the simple one-story building that served as living quarters for the Franciscans. A door swung unevenly on its hinges and startled them.

MacSweeney lifted Hugh to the sill of one of the small windows cut high in the wall.

"What do you see?"

"Nothing. It's deserted like all the others."

They crept stealthily into the rectory and made a room by room search. There was abundant evidence that the English had been here, that they had left in a hurry, and, indeed, that they intended to return. Beds were unmade and personal equipment was strewn about the wooden floor. A little pet dog yipped at the searchers.

Hugh came to one door that was locked. He kicked it open. Inside he saw the same general disorder as in the other compartments but piled high in the corner were bags of gold, chalices, and valuables which had been stripped from the chapel and other priceless objects which had been wrested from the people of Donegal.

Hugh drew his forehead into a tight frown. "This would be the room of Captain Leeds," he said, "or I've misjudged my man."

MacSweeney started to say something further but checked himself, realizing that this feud was personal and would welcome no assistance.

They took a quick look at the church, with similar results. The place had been torn and desecrated. Horses had been stabled here and the alien troops had marred the interior almost beyond recognition as a place of worship. MacSweeney swore a terrible oath and then steadied his temper.

"It wouldn't be like them to leave without makin' a fuss," he said. "Maybe they know we're here and are waiting in ambush."

Hugh shook his head thoughtfully and rubbed his

chin. "I don't think so. There's some other reason. Well, come on. This place is enough to give ideas to a ghost. We'd best get back with the others."

At as rapid a pace as Hugh's feet would allow, they ran back to the waiting column. There they mounted again but did not move out.

"What do you make of it, old friend?" Hugh asked.

"My guess," MacSweeney said, "is that they're moving in on the castle in force. This may be the all-out assault they've been building up for days."

As if in support of his theory, a great shout was heard from the direction of the castle and the clatter of horses and siege equipment broke the silence of the dawn. The periodic pounding of the small English cannon and the return fire of the Donegal guns rose above the fury of the onslaught.

"That's it!" Hugh shouted. "The attack is under way. Forward on the double!"

The sun had just come up over the ramparts of the castle as Hugh and his lieutenant rode up. Two artillery pieces were bombarding the main gate and a fire raft burned darkly in the moat. A siege tower lay crumpled at the edge of the water and another was moving into place along the east bank. Part of the moat had been filled with rock and English soldiers, their heads beneath their shields, were carrying scaling ladders up to the stout walls. From the battlements, the men and the women of Donegal poured spear and arrow and flaming liquid into the ranks of the insurgents. Their tiny ships' cannon dropped shells into the combat teams forming for the assault. But the English moved relentlessly on.

"Get the guns," Hugh commanded, and Mac-Sweeney signaled his small cavalry unit to follow him. Hugh led his kern and gallowglasses up the stone causeway to the very base of the fortress where the enemy infantry was massing for the scaling attempt.

The sudden attack from an unknown quarter threw the English into panic. This was enough to enable MacSweeney to ride down the gun crews and disable their instruments of war. Hugh, too, succeeded in closing with the invaders before they could group to defend themselves.

The terrible axmen of Swilly executed swift vengeance on the English. In broad sweeps they severed the feet of the scaling ladders and tumbled the besiegers into the midst of the bloody conflict. Grim pikemen moved forward in procession, catching the enemy on the points of their lances and hacking away at their crumbling lines. Hugh was everywhere—shouting commands, encouraging the infantry, engaging in a dozen sharp, personal encounters. Finally the English line broke and the scattered host fell back upon the main British camp. Here their capable commander, Sir Richard Bingham, succeeded in rallying them. They were fewer now but they still outnumbered the Irish and the element of surprise was no longer in the defenders' favor.

MacSweeney and his mounted men returned to Hugh's side.

"They're ready for us now but they're not over the first attack," Hugh called. "Take your horsemen along this bank of the river and hit them on the flank while we thrust at this broad front."

MacSweeney wheeled his little body of cavalry to the south and grouped them for assault.

The English had drawn up their troops behind a makeshift breastwork and began to direct a stream of arrows against the Irish. From the castle came an answering fire and the archers of the queen drew back. The English cavalry, superior in numbers and in equipment to MacSweeney's task force, was in the saddle and awaiting the command of its burly captain. At this moment the Irish moved against them.

Hugh's attack was not planned nor was it particularly skillful, but it had the advantage of a brave young man in the lead and a fearless army of disciplined warriors to follow him. Even the citizenry of Ballyshannon took heart and moved to the conflict like veterans. As they swept across the open space in front of the castle some dropped with arrows jutting from their bodies but the rest plunged on like a tide engulfing the waiting beach. Soon they had reached the breastwork and Hugh vaulted his steed to the top, catching the blade of an ax on his bright shield and replying with a blow from his broadsword. The Irish swarmed across the earthen barricade and engaged the enemy hand to hand. Locked in that

struggle they fought with every skill at their command and the English, knowing their fate lay in
their ability to ward them off, replied with equal
vigor. An arrow felled Hugh's mount and he pitched
to the ground still gripping his sword and shield. He
looked up to see the cruel face of Leeds staring
down at him. The captain was perched aboard a
fiery mare. No words were spoken. No cries of rage
or hatred exchanged. Leed's mouth opened in a fear-
ful grimace and his sword crashed down upon the
prince who had just risen to his knees. The impact
sent him reeling and Leeds was upon him attempt-
ing to crush him beneath the hooves of his mount.
But Hugh rolled away from this danger and scrambled to his feet. At that moment, however, a new
wave of the English entered the engagement and
separated the two mortal foes. Hugh had work of an
immediate nature to contend with as he cut a path
before him. Leeds sprang off at the head of a sudden cavalry charge.

MacSweeney had joined in the attack and had
driven his men to the rim of the British encamp-
ment. Here they were met by the English cavalry
and, though they fought bravely, they were driven
back to the bank of the river. The northern chieftain, too, was unhorsed but directed his men on foot,
dodging beneath the pike thrusts and bright arcing
swords of the enemy. Leeds pressed his advantage
with this unit and fed the river with the blood of
the clansmen. Nor could Hugh and his men come

to their aid. They were gripped in a fatal struggle with the desperate occupants of the stronghold.

The prince hobbled among his troops, guiding their slackening offense, and he began to realize that the issue was very much in doubt. It was his plan that Henry O'Neill should be signaled only when the enemy line had begun to falter and had fallen back to their small boats. Instead he found his own troops fighting for survival and he determined to signal the fleet immediately. But he could not fight his way clear to contact one of his archers. A savage blow smashed his helmet and sent him rolling in the mud. In an instant he was on his feet, helmetless, and his flaming red hair flashing wildly. The Irish attack had now stalled and the English were beginning to roll them back by the strength of their numbers. Suddenly help appeared from another source!

The great drawbridge of Donegal Castle fell with a crash and, led by the Dark Lady, the followers of O'Donnell streamed across, shouting the ancient battle cry, "O'Donnell to Victory!" They poured into the breach and attacked the English on their exposed flank. The bewildered foreigners turned to face the new onslaught and found themselves engaged on three sides and the river at their backs. MacSweeney's horsemen were relieved also by the appearance of some fresh cavalry from the castle who bore down on the English troops and sent them writhing back upon the eager Irish remnants. Caught in the center of this mounting conflagration of steel and shaft, the soldiers of the queen gave ground and began to initiate a desperate attempt to cut their way to the wharf and the waiting longboats.

Hugh took this opportunity to snatch the bow and quiver from a fallen English archer. To the point of his arrow he added a strip from his ragged tunic, set it afire by touching it to the flaming shell of a disabled cannon, and sent it in a high arc out over the bay. Even before it disappeared, hissing, into the sea, Henry O'Neill was on his way.

The startled English vessels let the Irish ships pass and offered them no resistance. Right to the wharf they sailed, shattering the waiting longboats as they closed in and tumbling their oarsmen into the mouth of the river. Then, led by the son of the great O'Neill and Martin, the bard of Cloghan, they beached their craft, spilled over the sides, and charged into a battleground already rent with the cries of the North countrymen and the sickening moans of the wounded and the dying. The fierce conflict raged all along the bank of the river and down to the narrow beach. The black and white landscape was now fused with the blood of both armies. But the issue was no longer in doubt. The Irish cavalry had disposed of the English horsemen and had joined the kern and gallowglasses against the ground troops. Thrown into confusion, the English broke and ran—right into the waiting arms of O'Neill and Martin and their fresh force off the boats. The British commander, grievously wounded himself, called upon his men to throw down their arms and,

amid the sorrowful sound of their obedience, he sur-
rendered to Red Hugh.

The boy was searching for one face in that throng
but did not see it. Perhaps Leeds had fallen earlier
in the battle. But his heart told him this was not so.
As he accepted the sword of Sir Richard Bingham,
his thoughts were elsewhere. He rushed about the
field like one possessed, peering at the bodies of the
shattered invaders. Suddenly he stopped.

"Of course!" he said aloud. "Of course! That's it!
He'd have ridden back there."

The prince grabbed the bridle of a riderless horse
and sprang into the saddle. He spurred past Ineen
Duive who was cantering over to greet him and past
the tired MacSweeney who watched him with a look
of amazement.

Hugh drove his horse across the soggy earth straight
toward the monastery, vaulting stiles that barred his
path and splashing through the miniature bogs that
rolled beneath him. He was well into the abbey yard
before he reined in and jumped to the ground. He
adjusted his shield on his left arm and let the weight
of his sword sink into his right. His red hair waving
in the breeze, he stepped across to the rectory where
the horse of Captain Leeds waited patiently.

Something plopped at his feet and he recognized
it as a shaft from a crossbow. He threw up his shield
in time to catch a second bolt and send it spinning
slowly against the chapel. Looking up he saw Leeds
reloading his weapon inside the monks' quarters and

he dashed for the shelter of the wide doorway. Then he kicked the portal open with his foot and leaped into the hall. Down the corridor he moved noiselessly with his shield before him and his broad blade at the ready. Another bright missile zipped by his ear and thudded into the paneled woodwork. He saw Leeds, ten paces away, taking aim once again and he dropped to the floor as the short arrow flew harmlessly over his head and out into the empty courtyard.

In a trice he was on his feet and running toward his foe. Leeds hurled the crossbow at him and momentarily checked his advance. In this instant, the Englishman had the opportunity to secure his own sword and buckler and he waited at the top of a three-step staircase for the attack. Hugh was on him just as he slid the shield into place and he parried the first slash with his own blade. With one foot on the first step, Hugh cut at his opponent with every trick at his command. He drew blood from Leeds' thigh and one of his strokes gashed the captain's head and caused him to shake it to clear his vision. But this was no one-sided encounter. Leeds was an excellent swordsman, not so skilled, perhaps, as Hugh, but stronger and doubly dangerous now that he was cornered.

The English officer moved to the attack and rained a series of shattering blows upon the shield of Red Hugh. Down the long hall he drove the prince, not striking him vitally but making the steel ring. Hugh rode with the blows, parried them, saved his strength, but Leeds did not seem to tire. He struck out savagely, swinging harshly from overhead, sneaking in from beneath, and cracking across the blade of the prince whenever it streaked out to meet his. Chips of metal flew as Leeds chopped away and soon he had Hugh in the doorway of the rectory. He lunged as if to take him in the side and then whipped his sword up and drove it down upon Hugh's upraised shield. Hugh fell with the shock and rolled into the court. Leeds struck at him once and buried his sword point in the mud. This gave Hugh his chance to recover and he was on his feet once more. Both men circled, breathing heavily. The wind had picked up and was drawing eerie sounds from the courtyard and chapel bells. Frightened birds screeched above the fight scene, and a pair of gaunt-looking vultures which had left their comrades at the bloody fields circled nearby.

In the open air, Hugh regained the advantage. He was quicker and his nimble blade darted above and beneath the shield of the Englishman, inflicting a dozen small wounds on his body. Striking back, Leeds hacked at his wiry opponent but he could not land. He began to stagger under the pain of his wounds and the wasted power of his own empty swings. They slithered about before the church steps, their blows ringing dissonantly with the bell above.

The wind was calling an absent congregation to church while the only living beings in the place sought gravely to put one another to death.

Hugh felt the chapel's steps against his heel and stepped up with his left foot, lunging at the same instant. The thrust caught Leeds in the side once more and he bellowed like an enraged animal. With all the brute strength of his massive frame, he swung his blade, caring little for the science of movement, and split Hugh's shield in two. Encouraged, he swung again, but Hugh turned aside and the steel smashed into the rock stairs with a clang. Before the echo of this blow had died, Hugh's own sword descended to meet the taut neck of the captain. In that downward flight, all the anger and all the bitterness descended, too, and fell to earth with the bulky form of the captain. Leeds was dead, taking away with him all the fearsome memories of Birmingham Tower.

The chapel bell tolled unevenly and the circling vultures landed on the sloping roof of the rectory.

chapter 18

THE PRINCE SANK to one knee and felt all the weariness of the busy day creep upon him. He barely felt it when MacSweeney picked him up in his great arms and seated him on his horse. The short ride cleared his head, though, and before he reached Donegal, something of a reawakening had taken place and he faced the field of slaughter as one who had emerged from a dream. If this were true—if it were a dream—then certainly the Dark Lady was an angel who rode slowly and proudly up to meet the hero who had engineered this decisive defeat.

When the two met, it was like the fusing of two spirits, like the "Meeting of the Waters" in Avonbeg where the gentle streams mingle. All the misery of the four years was forgotten in that embrace and all the bravado of the heroic morning melted into simple tears as mother and son were reunited. Around them lay the horror of war but in their hearts only joy reigned and, together, the mother on a slow, ambling horse and the son, limping, with his hand on the bridle, re-entered Donegal Castle.

While the warriors busied themselves with the wounded, MacSweeney rounded up the English prisoners and herded them before Hugh and his mother. The O'Donnells were sitting in the courtyard resting and Hugh was about to pay a visit to the king when MacSweeney interrupted him.

"What shall we do with our prisoners?" he asked with a sly wink.

Hugh studied the frightened men before him. Visions of his torments at the hands of the English rose up like the foul smell from the bloody arena. All of the bitterness he had locked in his heart surged up, and as quickly disappeared.

"Take them to the longboats and show them the way to Dublin," he replied at last.

"You're going to let them go?"

"Yes. Are we not taught to forgive our enemies?"

The queen smiled. Long had been her thoughts of what Birmingham Tower would do to her son. Now she was reassured.

Not all of the enemy were grateful for the reprieve. Sir Richard Bingham, the defeated commander, stepped forth haughtily.

"It is possible we shall meet again, Red Hugh O'Donnell."

"I hope, if this is so, the results will be the same." The Irish chuckled at the jest and MacSweeney slapped his broad thigh with a roar.

Though flustered, Bingham continued, "The queen of England has many men at arms. We are but a small part of her force. Her armies will seek you out, will hunt you down and revenge today's insult."

The prince rose, his face livid with rage. "Now you hear me," he declared, "and so inform your queen. Red Hugh O'Donnell and O'Neill of Tyrone are in alliance together. With us are MacSweeney and Maguire and soon the O'Reilly and the O'Hagan and the other clans of the North. It is we that shall do the hunting and you shall be our prey. We shall not rest until we have driven the English before us into the sea. If you choose to visit us again, Sir Richard, the fates may not be so kind nor the O'Donnells so tolerant." He paused, regained his composure, and then waved the group away with his hand.

MacSweeney gave Bingham a none-too-gentle shove and started the prisoners toward the boats. They were required to take their wounded and their dead with them. The latter would be buried at sea, dropping like stones into the channel that separated their homes and the alien land where destiny overtook them.

Tenderly the Irish soldiers carried their own dead to the Donegal cemetery. The monks were returning now and would prepare them for burial. Throughout that night the coffinmakers would be at their grim hammering and many a weeping woman would bring forth from her closet the winding sheet in which to lay her son or husband. For these saddened few the glory of the morning was short-lived.

MacSweeney, protesting, was led away to the castle

infirmary, to be treated along with the other wounded.

"By the piper of Moses!" he bellowed. "It's not but a little scratch on the leg and a fair whack on the skull. Let me be, now!" But they half-pushed and half-dragged the old warrior to the makeshift hospital where his wounds were pronounced not too serious.

"Sure, and I told them that, good Father," he shouted, swinging his arm for emphasis. "The curse of the crows upon ye all!"

The attendants all laughed heartily as MacSweeney stormed out of the place and the little medical monk, aghast, looked on high and crossed himself.

Hugh took leave of his mother, promising to return in a moment. Then he climbed the familiar stairs to his father's chamber, limping as he went. His knock sounded back in his memory, through time and torment, to the day when last his trembling fist struck against the same wood.

A feeble voice called, "Come in, my boy," and Hugh entered his father's room.

How the poor man has changed, thought Hugh. The king's face was more drawn than ever, the thin frame wasted and the outstretched hand unsteady. There were tears of gratitude in his eyes.

"My boy, my boy." The king took Hugh's hand in his own.

"I am home, father. Home to stay."

"Ah, yes. You've had many adventures. All Donegal

speaks of your courage and your faith. Well do I know that without you we'd have lost the province and all we've striven to keep these long years."

Hugh smiled kindly on his father and said, "Sure now, you'd have figured a way to stop them, sir. No enemy has entered but as a prisoner since you were born in this castle."

The father shook his head. "No," he said, "before you left I deceived myself into believing that I should again rule over the clan of O'Donnell."

"And you will, father, you will!"

"Let me continue, boy. This is not to be. I am now scarce able to sit up, let alone ride a horse or lead an army. There will be days ahead that call for that. No, my son, the crown must pass. The future of the O'Donnell now lies in your hands. When we have tended our wounded and buried our dead, we shall name a new chieftain, one, I trust, whose deed shall be written larger than those of any O'Donnell since time began."

"I am not unscathed myself," Hugh protested, looking down at his injured foot. "I am lamed, father, and shall not again walk with the grace that befits a ruler."

Old Hugh tapped his own thin chest. "Arrah, grace is here, son," he said. "You are a king, never fear, and the wound one suffers at the hands of the enemy need not bar him from the kingship. Rather should they exalt him to it. Aye, exalt him to it." He nodded as if pleased with his own philosophy.

The prince paused and then began, "Father—!"

"Please, Hugh, do not attempt to humor an old man. Go now. There is much to do and we have the years ahead to talk."

The prince got up slowly, kissed his father on the forehead, and sadly, but proudly, left the room.

Downstairs his mother was waiting for him. And she had a guest.

"Now Hugh," she chided him. "Is that any way to greet Kathleen and she after riding the better part of the day to be with you?"

The brave warrior of the morning had no words for this situation. All he could do was gulp and say, "Kathleen, you—you look more lovely than ever." It was the speech he had planned to say when they met but somehow it sounded strange and inept now.

Blushing a little, Kathleen walked over to Hugh and took his arm. In all of his distorted dreams in Dublin, in all of his daytime longings, the young man had never been able to do justice to her beauty. Now, thrilled by his return, Kathleen took a radiance which not even Martin could capture with his sweet words and mellow voice. Her long black tresses, her proud carriage, her twinkling gray eyes—in all of Ireland, thought Hugh, there is not another like her.

At that moment the elder MacSweeney came bursting upon the scene, his head swathed in bandages and his dark beard nearly singed with the fury of his anger.

"By the contents of all the books that were ever

opened and shut," he shouted, "they're a bunch of thievin' devils who'd have me heart in that black hospital of a place." Seeing the two young lovers he stopped short. Hugh and Kathleen seemed not to hear. The grizzled veteran scratched his throbbing head.

The Dark Lady signaled him to steal quietly away and away he went, casting back a half-puzzled, half-pleased look.

Hugh led Kathleen up the stairs of the main tower and out onto the battlements that overlooked the Bay of Donegal. A huge gull fluttered above them and then dived down to the black rocks that supported the west wall of the fortress. Across the wide expanse of the Atlantic they could see the departure of the English fleet. A far circle of mountains cupped the gold-tinged waters of the bay like a goblet of a king. For the first time in many hours, in many months actually, a hush of perfect peace came over Donegal as if some silent harper had lulled the world to a whisper.

When Kathleen spoke it was to ask about Hugh's wound.

"It is nothing," he said with a bit of a boast. "An inconvenience, nothing more."

"Oh, Hugh!" Kathleen suddenly tightened her grip on Hugh's arm. "It is so good to have you back."

The prince looked down on her beautiful, serious face and saw a tear leaving the corner of each eye.

"Here now," he said. "That's no way to act. I'll

think you want me back in Dublin." He offered her his handkerchief. "Here. Blow your nose."

Kathleen stamped her foot. "Oh, you can never be serious!" She looked him straight in the eye and drew herself up to her full height. "Red Hugh O'Donnell, I love you and I mean to marry you if I have to wait another four years, or four times four, before you make up your mind."

"Well, now, Kathleen MacSweeney, so that's your plan is it? I cannot see how any man could hold out long against such a scheme."

Hugh kissed her lightly on the lips and then she clung to him with her eyes pinched shut as if to keep out the least sight that might disturb the moment.

For the remainder of the day Hugh took command, ordering a cleanup of the battle area, repairing the defense of the castle, seeing to the lodging of his friends and neighbors who had assisted him in battle. MacSweeney, still grumbling, was permitted to visit with his old friend, Red Hugh's father, and he painted for the old man the entire story of the battle for Donegal. Martin, who was with him, filled in the details of the flight north. The elder O'Donnell could not get enough of their stories. He begged them to repeat whole episodes and questioned them over and over about the brave conduct of his son. It was not until his wife put her foot down that the two old cronies stole away, leaving the king to his much-needed rest.

Hugh spent a full hour or more looking out the window of his room into the dark bay and he breathed a prayer of thanks for the Divine Providence which had seen him through his many adventures. Finally he crept to his bed and was asleep when the sentry called, "Twelve o'clock and all is well."

The next day and the one after were filled with duties pertaining to the soldier dead. Hugh and his mother followed behind the long line of coffins borne to the graveyard by the dead ones' families. The sad keen of the women accompanied the heroes on their last journey and filled the countryside with one great sound of weeping. With heads bowed, Hugh and the other chieftains stood by the separate graves while the monks prayed over them and blessed them.

"*Requiescant in pace,*" they intoned.

And Donegal said, "*Amen.*"

When the melancholy ordeal was over, the elder O'Donnell announced that it was time for his son to succeed him as the leader of the clan. His command was met with rejoicing for the prince was well loved and the warriors of the North were eager to serve again under a general in the field.

The day of the inauguration dawned serene and beautiful. A warm sun had been at work for several days and the earth had begun to peer out from beneath the blanket of snow. With his proud and solemn mother on one side and his aged father in a litter on the other, the handsome young prince stood resolutely upon the Rock of Doone, the memorial throne of the O'Donnell, and accepted the wand of leadership. It was white to signify his authority and the purity and steadfastness that must characterize his rule. In honor of the Holy Trinity he turned thrice from left to right and thrice from right to left, looking as he did so at the Bay of Donegal, the white-capped mountains, and the fertile black fields that marked the limits of his kingdom. Erect and with regal bearing, he heard Martin, the inaugurator, shout out, "O'Donnell!" thus assigning to him a title higher than any of the foreigners could give, the ancient title of his ancestors, the chiefs of Donegal. And each man among the high officials, according to rank, cried out, "O'Donnell!" and the voices of hundreds of clansmen carried "O'Donnell!" far into the distance. MacSweeney and his men shook their broad axes on high; Henry O'Neill and Martin sang forth the name; Kathleen breathed it with tenderness; and a mother and father wept at the sound of it.

It spread like a spear across Donegal, reverberated in the vastness of the northern slopes, dipped to appraise the clear blue waters of the Atlantic, circled, with a blessing, each village and town of the province, and came back again to settle like an echo of tomorrow on the bright flaming head of Red Hugh O'Donnell.

living history library

The *Living History Library* is a collection of works for children published by Bethlehem Books, comprising quality reprints of historical fiction and non-fiction, including biography. These books are chosen for their craftsmanship and for the intelligent insight they provide into the present, in light of events and personalities of the past.

TITLES IN THIS SERIES

about the author

Robert (Bob) T. Reilly was born in Lowell, Massachusetts in 1923. During World War II, he enlisted in the Army and saw service as a First lieutenant with the 78th Division in Europe. He was a POW for six months, and received numerous decorations. After the war Reilly completed his Ph.D. at Boston University.

Reilly's Irish interests involve the American Committee for Irish studies and the Irish American Cultural Institute, where he held a national directorship. Reilly has lived in Ireland and has also led tours there since 1966.

It was when he was teaching Irish Literature at Creighton University in Omaha, Nebraska, that he had the inspiration to write *Red Hugh*. "I did it as a bet with myself that I could write a book," he recalls. His first attempt at the story of Hugh O'Donnell was rejected by a publisher, so he tossed the manuscript out and started over. This time the tale was successful and became the first of several historical fiction books the author has written.

After the war Reilly married Jean McKenzie of Omaha, Nebraska, where he now resides. He is the father of ten children, three sons and seven daughters, and has seventeen grandchildren. Reilly is still actively writing, and is working on, among other things, a history of Irish pubs.